EVP Lab 1.0

My Failures & Success in Recording
Electronic Voice Phenomenon

About the Author

Dr. John D. Gruber Ph.D. (Columbus, Ohio), was pushed into the world of paranormal activity starting at age 4 when he began to see and hear shadow people invading his bedroom at night. These events terrified and tormented him until the age of 15 when it all just seemed to stop. Three years later, after graduating from Galion Senior High School in Galion Ohio, he attended The Ohio State University to take courses in the field of nursing anesthesia. During his first year, he fell in love with psychology due largely to his instructor, Marge Haslett who encouraged him to take a more extensive look at the field, and he changed his major. In 2007 through 2009, he enrolled in parapsychology courses and achieved his diploma. He enjoys music, photography, writing, and audio/visual analysis and editing. He is also the director of an active EVP research team, SPATS serving Columbus, and Central Ohio.

To Write to the Author

If you wish to contact Dr. John D. Gruber Ph. D. or would like more information about this book, write to:

Dr. John D. Gruber Ph.D. In care of SPATS

2764 Vanderberg Ave.

Columbus, Ohio 43204-2704, U.S.A.

Or browse the internet at SPATSINFO.com and Click on the e-mail link from the web sites home page.

EVP Lab 1.0

My Failures & Success in Recording

Electronic Voice Phenomenon

Dr. John D. Gruber Ph. D.

First Edition 2010

Book Design by Dr. John D. Gruber

Cover Design by Dr. John D. Gruber

Cover Photo © 2007 by SPATS, Columbus, OH

ISBN 978-0-557-33151-2

ISBN 978-0-557-33151-2

90000

9 780557 331512

Dedication & Thanks

My sincere gratitude and thanks go to many individuals, whose help and input has made this book possible;

My wife Linda S. Gruber for putting up with me throughout,

Dennis W. Hauck for helping me out with white noise research,

My grandmother Helen Latimore for her unconditional love,

Konstantin Raudive for his constant search for the truth and inspiration to guide me in theory and practical application,

To Jacob for his complete un-wavering inner guidance,

And to all those dedicated to the field of research in Electronic Voice Phenomenon (EVP) and Instrumental Trans Communication (ITC) recordings.

And I dedicate this book to;

My Grandchildren, Ashley, Siera, Melody and Robert

Dr. John D. Gruber Ph. D.

March 1st, 2010

Contents

Introduction

How and Why did I get Interested in EVP?

I had traumatic events each and every time the lights went out for the night in my childhood home in Galion Ohio. My parents were beside themselves and my adopted sister would yell and tease me relentlessly about interrupting her comfortable nights of sleeping bliss. I was a very nervous, jumpy 6 year old, that let every older kid beat the heck out of me cause I had low self esteem, embarrassed because my sister has told them everything, and besides, I know they heard my father swear at me every morning about losing his much needed rest due to my vivid imagination and screaming outbursts during the night before.

I got great grades from my teachers in elementary school, and I enjoyed the time in class, as long as the end of the day bell didn't ring. You see, when that bell rang, I had to head for home and begin the start of what was nothing short of a long journey into terror that would only end as the sun came up the next morning.

I would get home, complete my homework, grab a snack and watch T.V. until my parents got home around 6pm. My parents owned their own Carpet and Linoleum business downtown Galion and in Bucyrus for over 38 years, mom ran the store while my father installed the goods. They were hard working people and quickly became well known throughout the town. Well, mom would fix dinner and we would sit down to it, although I would get increasingly fidgety, and anxious, because bed time was 8 o'clock, just a few hours after dinner, and I would begin to wonder what the wee hours of the morning would have in store for me this time.

I had a ritual that I followed to the T. First bath, pajamas, and teeth, then find the thickest blanket in the laundry, if it wasn't in my room already, and say a prayer, a long prayer to help me live through the night.

I felt that the prayer never helped me very much, but wanted to keep my options open with God anyway, in case I would be joining him that evening. I always tried to find excuses to keep my bedroom and the hall lights on, at least up to the bathroom, as long as I could. Some nights, my parents would not notice or care that the light was on and I got a good restful night. But mostly, they would yell, to make me turn them off immediately, and my Dagwood Bumsted plan would go into action. I would start at the bath and then make a run for it to my room, hitting switches on the fly till I could sail into my bed and under the covers safely.

Usually at first I would finally drift off to sleep, but would always be awakened by the first unfamiliar noise or lack of moonlight through my window where the just was some. I just knew it was them, I could just feel it, and it was too easy to tell, way too easy. Sometimes I would hear faint whispers, but mostly the shadow movement around the bedroom, or closet door would catch my eye first, progressing to the foot or edge of my bed. I would cover my head and freeze right where I was, to no avail, they would still whisper to me, "help us", and "please help us" and at times they would talk to a Kenneth, whom I assumed was another spirit or shadow person in my room. I found out later on in life quite by accident that my given name was Kenneth. I went in to the doctor's office when I needed to have a surgical procedure done, and was asked questions about my family medical history. I always defaulted to "I'm adopted, I have no family history. The doctor got upset with me and told me that I could have my records all I needed to do was go to the court house in Crawford County and get them. Well, I did and paid my $2 and got my original birth certificate. And to my amazement, there was my family's medical history and my given name. Kenneth Lynn Ricks. Things were beginning to make some sense.

The images I could get away from with my thick blanket, the insistent voices I could not, even when I had pre-cottoned my ears. I didn't have a tape recorder in the early 60's so I don't know if I could have caught the voices for proof or not, but it didn't matter to my parents, because I was just nuts, "no one is in this house but you and us", my father would say, "you have got to stop this lying and making up people in your room at night to get attention". As some readers of a certain age know, back then to get you to mind and comply, there was a bit of yard stick, belt and ping pong paddle action going on, enough said about that.

Even after moving into a new home on Portland Way South, across town when I was about 9 the shadow people never stopped. They never skipped a beat, they just wanted to communicate with me, but I took it as they wanted to haunt me, scare me, torture and kill me.

Where was Chip Coffey when I needed him, Oh yeah, let's see, I am older than him so he wasn't born yet, therefore, not available. Rats!

Children can see things that adults can't, although you should remember those imaginary friends and ghosts in your closet when you were a little tike, and take those, not so good memories to heart when you are dealing with a child that might be having the same reaction to spirits visiting during the lonely night in his or her bedroom. We are finding more and more the level of awareness children have to spiritual events, so let's have a little more compassion, courage, love and understanding for our precious kids that might be having the scariest event of their lives. It is possible that your child is not lying or making up stories just to get attention. It may be someone else is trying to get your child's attention.

Well, to let you know how things turned out, the spooky stuff stopped at about the age of 14. My life settled down for a good long time, I got married, Mathew was born, my first child. I went to college full time and worked full time as a night welder at Carter Mfg. in Galion. A year or two later I entered into the nurse anesthetist program at The Ohio State University and worked as an EMT and orderly at the Galion Community Hospital. In a short while two more children were born, Melissa and Heather, my beautiful daughters. While attending my classes at the Marion Ohio branch of OSU, I met Marge Haslett an instructor for the psychology department, and I became more and more fascinated with her program rather than the nursing aspect I signed up for. I changed majors in 1975 from nursing to the psychology field and have stayed the course ever since. Then I met a psychic in 2003, and my life direction changed again.

It was amazing how he could know the things in my life that had taken place way before he was even born, I am at least 20 years his senior, but he knew things I had done or seen, and some were really off the wall things that I had put off in my mind in that "who cares", place we all have. Never the less, he was spot on with his assessment of my youthful fears, concerns and traumatic events in the night, and convinced me to further my education in parapsychology to help me find the truth and meaning to what I had experienced and to open the door to spirituality in my life.

I then proceeded to peruse the internet looking for answers on EVP's, ghosts, paranormal, spirits and certifications, classes or seminars in all levels of paranormal events. I purchased several books by Richard Southall, Loyd Auerbach, Jeff Belanger, Paul Roland, and Troy Taylor.

I joined a slew of organizations dealing with the paranormal on the internet and became most intrigued with the voices of the dead, EVP's and ITC. I then came across Flamel College and inquired about the online classes as an

EVP technician. I said what the heck; I will take all the classes as they have them mapped out in the course study guide online and get another diploma in something I am interested in. So I proceeded to enroll and found it cheap as dirt when compared to other online courses. I enjoyed the paranormal investigator, advanced investigator and the EVP technician courses and have a certificate in each, but it was the EVP course study that got to me the most, hit a nerve so to speak, and to find out that Thomas Jefferson was working on a spirit communicator until his death, the Vatican was and still is interested in the communication with the afterlife, interested enough to spend time and funds on research projects? Oh yeah! I murmured, this was for me; this was the research study avenue I wanted to pursue because it most summed up life growing up, messages from the dead, from the shadows in my bedroom to a recorder in my lab. Outstanding!

I couldn't wait to get started so I began purchasing books, magazines, news articles and once again hit the internet. But, to my surprise each and every piece of reading material, research topic, or EVP study group I came across had as many different opinions of what would work and what won't than there are fish in the sea. Many of them conflicted in such a huge manner, it was obvious I was going to have to try each and every method until I attained my own results, and then refine a method till I get where I want to be, yet still conscious of my budget. I met Evan an employee at a local Sam Ash music store to inquire about some recording equipment, microphones, stands and the like, and found out that another employee was a paranormal investigator in a local group. The two of them helped me out immensely and answered a lot of questions that I know they don't get on a daily basis. Now I had my own investigative group, SPATS with hand held digital recorders, EMF, K2 meters and night vision video equipment. I don't really get excited over dust orbs and old house settling noises that everybody else thinks is paranormal activity, and I can't get excited over some of the completely garbled alien sounding, scratchy noise so they have to make up something they think the spirit might have said EVP's either.

Did it just say "march up the hill" or "Marsha take your pill", who knows! It could have been "Martian at the mill" for all I know. Nothing what so ever was discernable to me, not one thing sounded like a word or sentence. I know I couldn't be the only one out there that didn't hear a thing. With that type of clarity the supposed voice or sound could have sounded like or said anything. I have heard some of the so called captured EVPs on the sound files of other research groups over the internet and YouTube and unless I am completely def or have ear muffs on, I don't hear it. It's not clear, it sounds like a cat moaning and then they tell me it says "get out", what get out? I definitely don't hear that anywhere. I hear an old time record scratching or some Star Trek echo sound effect that makes no sense at all. So, I decided that for this type of research to be worth any contribution for the paranormal coming into the light of the real world, I need studio quality recording equipment with all the trimmings to capture the disembodied voices sounding like just another person in the room. To me, these sounds that some people are all in a tizzy about, calling them messages from beyond, sound like background noise effects from a Sponge Bob episode. I wanted to be different; I wanted to be the guy that gets the best communication possible from the other side. I want to carry on with Konstantin Raudive's work. This is my quest, and this book is the failure and success of my research into communicating with spirits thus far. I hope you will find the way I have explained and done my research, and experiments that this would be something you could get interested in and climb aboard, it is after all, a fascinating journey into what may still be ahead of us. I find it very hard to believe that when we die there is nothing left, that's it, the big Kahuna. I believe that this just can't be folks, it just can't be, there has to be more to it than that. Well, at least I hope so.

Chapter One:

1

Research Abundance

Since the discovery of what is now known as 'Electronic Voice Phenomena' (EVP), we must give thanks for all the efforts of many gifted researchers who, over the years have given their time and commitment in the face of much hostility to its research.

Where did it all begin? Well, I believe with the discoveries made in the field of electronic communications by inventers such as Thomas Edison, Nikola Tesla, Oliver Lodge and Guglielmo Marconi. These men of vision all held belief in an afterlife and the possibility of making contact with that world through electronic means. Edison had his first lab at the age of ten and by the time of his death he had patented 1093 of his inventions. He also believed in a 'life after death', as can be determined by the many statements he made during his lifetime. In support of this, what follows is just one of them "I will be going to a world beyond, whereby I shall continue the research where I left off". It is also interesting to note that there was a blueprint found after his death for a machine which he believed could be used for making contact with that very place. As no machine was ever found, we have no means of knowing if he had actually built this, although there is proof positive he was working on the Spiricom after the death of his wife. More of this evidence to his belief in the afterlife was stated in the following quote;

"I am inclined to believe that our personality hereafter will be able to affect matter. If we can evolve an instrument so delicate as to be affected by our personality as it survives in the next life, such an instrument, ought to record something." –Thomas Edison

A bit of history about EVP, now I am not going to bore you with long drawn out biographies about the early pioneers of this research so don't worry, but I feel you must be informed about the most important parts so here goes. Actually, it is not so ancient history, rather it is relatively new and innovative. In 1928 Thomas Alva Edison wrote about his interest in the afterlife. The man, who invented the electric light bulb, motion picture camera, and the phonograph, was working with his assistant, Dr. Miller Hutchinson, in Edison's laboratory, building a machine in hopes of communicating with the spirits of the dead. Dr. Miller Hutchinson wrote of the experience, "Edison and I are convinced that in the fields of psychic research will yet be discovered facts that will prove of greater significance to the thinking of the human race than in all the inventions we have ever made in the field of electricity." Edison himself wrote, "If our personality survives, then it is strictly logical or scientific to assume that it retains memory, intellect, other faculties, and knowledge that we acquire on this earth." "Therefore, if we can evolve an instrument so delicate as to be affected by our personality as it survives in the next life, such an instrument, when made available, ought to record something." Edison also wrote about how to modify television sets and to tune them to 740 megahertz to receive paranormal images in communications. Unfortunately, Edison died before he could finish his greatest invention, a device called the "Spiricom", and since his death many researchers have attempted to build one. Even as he lay dying he told the physician, "It is very beautiful over there."

Numerous advances have been made in the development of the Spiricom, particularly through the encouragement and funding of American industrialist, George Meek, who in the 1970's, worked with a gifted psychic named William O'Neil and successful developed a version of the Spiricom device. It consisted, among other stuff, a set of 13 tone generators that allowed for the first time ever allegedly, actual dialog through electronic equipment between Heaven and Earth. Critics have argued that the entire experiment was a farce and to this day it cannot be confirmed or denied.

EVP as we now know it began in 1959 when Freidrich Jürgenson was recording birdsongs in the Swedish countryside. When he got home and played back the recordings, he distinctly heard mysterious Norwegian voices discussing nocturnal birdsongs. He also heard a female voice speaking in German say, "Friedrich, you are being watched. Friedel, my little Friedel, can you hear me?" Friedrich was completely convinced it was the voice of his dead mother. Jürgenson went on to record many other voices over the next four years before he went public with his claims and published two books: "Voices from the Universe" and "Radio Contact with the Dead," both of which are out of print. He had not heard these voices while he was recording the birds, but he clearly heard them at playback. Some voices even gave him detailed instructions on how to record more EVP Voices.

Hearing of Jürgenson's research, Dr. Konstantin Raudive a Latvian psychologist who taught at the University of Uppsala, Sweden, became obsessed with EVP research, and became the world's best known researcher in the field. He had recorded over 72 thousand EVPs during his life time and they still remain some of the finest recordings in the world.

In 1971, the chief engineers of Pye Record Ltd. decided to test Raudive's claims and ran a controlled experiment with Raudive. They invited him to their sound lab and installed special equipment to block out any radio and television signals. Raudive was not allowed to touch any of the equipment. Raudive used one tape recorder that was monitored by the studio's control tape recorder. They taped Raudive speaking into the microphone for over eighteen minutes and not one person or monitor picked up any other sounds. But when the scientists played back the tape, to their amazement, they had recorded over 200 unexplainable voices.

That same year, Raudive released some of his recordings on a 7-inch vinyl record together with a book titled' 'The Inaudible Becomes Audible." The book was published in an expanded English edition as, "Breakthrough: An Amazing Experiment in Electronic Communication with the Dead."

Interestingly enough, the Vatican was very excited about Raudive's work and many high-ranking Vatican officials visited him to hear the voices. In September of 1952, two priests, Father Ernetti from Italy a respected authority in science, and a physicist and philosopher, and also a music lover, along with his colleague, Father Gemelli, the President of the Papal Academy, were recording a Gregorian Chant when a wire on their magneto phone kept breaking. Exasperated, Father Gemelli looked up and asked his deceased father for help. To the two men's astonishment, his father's voice was recorded on the magneto phone, answering, "Of course I shall help you, I'm always with you." They repeated the experiment and this time a very clear voiced filled with humor said, "But Zucchini, it is clear, don't you know it is I?" That was all the verification Father Gemelli needed, because nobody knew the nickname his father had teased him with when he was a young boy. The two men visited Pope Pius XII, [09] in Rome with the news of their breakthrough. The Pope stated to the men, "The existence of this voice is strictly a scientific fact and has nothing whatsoever to do with spiritualism." "The recorder is totally objective." "It receives and records only sound waves from wherever they come." "This experiment may perhaps become the cornerstone for a building of scientific studies which will strengthen people's faith in a hereafter."

The Vatican expressed a keen interest in EVP research ever since. Pope Paul VI [10] was kept informed of research being done from 1959 onwards by his good friend and EVP pioneer Friedrich Jürgenson; In fact, the Pope made Jürgenson a Knight Commander of the Order of St. Gregory in 1969 for his work in EVP. The Vatican also gave permission for priests to conduct their own research into EVP if they felt strong about it. Father Leo Schmid had actually been assigned a small parish in Oeschegen, Switzerland; in 1967 to give him time to experiment with recording the mysterious voices discovered By Father Ernetti and Father Gemelli. He collected more than 10 thousand voices, many of which were published in his book, 'When the dead Speak." posthumously in 1976.

And then in 1982, comes EVP researcher Sara Estep who founded the AAEVP, which among other things sponsors conferences that are held worldwide about EVP research. She had recorded over 20 thousand EVPs in her life time and had plenty of accounts to share. Sarah told us of one occasion when the famous EVP pioneer Dr. Konstantin Raudive actually called her on the phone in 1994, twenty years after his death. When a surprised Sarah heard the voice of her deceased colleague, she exclaimed, "Dr. Raudive, how are you?' and Konstantin replied, "I am fine as a dead one can be." "Dear Sarah, thank you for the work you have done…and the conversation continued from there on. Sarah passed on from this world January 3rd, 2008. AAEVP still moves ahead and is a great resource for your questions to be answered.

As you may already know, the internet is a plethora of knowledge when it comes to investigating the paranormal world and the capturing of disembodied voices, electronic voice phenomenon or Instrumental TransCommunication (ITC). Each group, research paper or book has an exclusive method of attaining and capturing spirit voices from the dead. Some of the best sites to gain information and for your reading pleasure are as follows; The American Association of Electronic Voice Phenomena (AA-EVP) founded by, Sarah Estep in 1982, Electronic voice phenomenon from Wikipedia, the free encyclopedia online, Konstantin Raudive published his first book, Breakthrough: An Amazing Experiment in Electronic Communication with the Dead in 1968 and it was translated into English in

1971 but this book if you find it will cost you a fortune so stick to some of the excerpts from it that are posted online, Von Szalay and Bayless' work was published by the Journal of the American Society for Psychical Research in 1959. Bayless later went on to co-author the 1979 book, Phone Calls from the Dead. And then there is always the Swedish painter and film producer Friedrich Jürgenson who in 1959 was recording bird songs. Upon playing the tape later, he heard what he interpreted to be his dead father's voice and then the spirit of his deceased wife calling out his name. He went on to make several more recordings; including one that he was convinced contained a message from his late mother. He authored (Voices from Space), published in Sweden in 1964.

Famous Author Sir Conan Doyle [16] was fascinated by the afterlife and was said to have written about it. After the death of his wife Louisa in 1906, and the death of his son Kingsley, Conan Doyle sank into depression. He found solace supporting spiritualism and its alleged scientific proof of existence beyond the grave. Sir Arthur became involved with Spiritualism to the extent that he wrote a Professor Challenger novel on the subject, The Land of Mist.

This is an EVP timeline of research that I could come up with so what follows is information of past and present researchers who we owe a debt of gratitude for the efforts they have given us to further our knowledge of this amazing discovery. (A few are pictured within Appendix A)

1920`s Hereward Carrington [01] Psychic Researcher begins experimenting.

1928 Thomas Edison [02] worked on equipment he hoped would permit communication with the dead, using a chemical apparatus with potassium permanganate.

1930`s The Scandinavian military pick up what was probably the first ever polygot messages. At the time believed to be German coded messages, which was later discounted.

1936 Attilz Von Szalay started to experiment with a Pack-Bell record-cutter and player, trying to capture paranormal voices on phonograph records.

1956 Raymond Bayless [03] joined Attliz Von Szalay in experiments and wrote an article for the Journal of the American Society for Psychical Research in 1959.

1959 Swedish film maker Friedrich Jürgenson [04] discovered strange voices while recording bird sounds.

1964 Jürgenson after 5 years of research publishes his findings in his book Roesterna Fraen Rymden (Voices from the Universe). Attliz Von Szalay gets voices of his deceased relatives on tape for the first time.

1965 Dr. Konstantin Raudive [05], a Latvian psychologist and philosopher, visited Juergenson, concluded that the phenomenon was genuine, and started his own experiments in Bad Krozingen, Germany.

1967 Thomas Edison spoke through West German clairvoyant Sigrun Seuterman, in trance, about his earlier efforts in 1928 to develop equipment for recording voices from the beyond. Edison also made suggestions as to how to modify TV sets and tune them to 740 megahertz to get paranormal effects. (Session recorded on tape by Paul Affolter, Liestal, Switzerland). Franz Seidi, Vienna, developed the "sychophone". Theodore Rudolph developed a goniometer for Raudive's experiments.

1968 Father Leo Schmid, Oeschegen, Switzerland, was assigned a small parish to give him time to experiment with taping voices. His book, Wen Die Toten Reden (When the Dead Speak) was published in 1976, shortly after his death. Raudive published his book Unhoerbares Wird Hoerbar (The Inaudible Becomes Audible); based on 72,000 voices he recorded.

1970 D. Scott Rogo [13] and Raymond Bayless [03] publish 'Phone Calls from the Dead'.

1970 Raymond Cass begins experimenting.

1971 Colin Smythe, Ltd. England, published explained English translations of Raudive's book: Breakthrough, an Amazing Experiment in Electronic Communication with the Dead. Marcello Bacci and co-workers in Grosseto, Italy, made weekly contact with 'spirit' communicators for their progress reports, which had still continued up to 1988. William Adams Welch publishes his findings 'Talks with the Dead'. Paul Jones, George W Meek and Hans Heckman, Americans, opened a laboratory. In which they implemented the first serious research to create a two-way voice communication system far more sophisticated than the equipment used in EVP approach.

1972 Gilbert Bonner, [15] a dedicated researcher who amassed a huge collection of voices during his lifetime, begins experimenting. Peter Bander, England, wrote Carry on Talking, published in U.S. as Voices from the Tapes.

1973 Josephand Michael Lamoreaux, Washington State, had success with recording paranormal voices after reading Raudive's book.

1975 The formation of V.T.F German research group. William Addams Welch, Hollywood script writer and playwright, authored Talks with the Dead.

1978 William O'Neil [14] working for George Meek, using a modified single side-band radio had brief, but evidential contact with an American medical doctor said to have died five years earlier.

1981 Manfred Boden has unsolicited contact with communicators of non-human evolution via a telephone and computer.

1982 George Meek [06] made a trip around the world to distribute tape recordings of 16 excerpts of communications between William O'Neil and an American scientist who died 14 years earlier. He also distributed a 100-page technical report giving wiring diagrams, photos, technical data and guidelines for research by others. Hans Otto Koenig, West Germany, develops sophisticated electronic equipment, using extremely low beat frequency oscillators, ultra-violet and infra-red lights, etc. Sarah Estep [11] begins the American Association of EVP (AA-EVP)

1984 Kenneth Webster, England, receives (via several different computers) 250 communications from a person who lived in the 16th century. Most print-outs are in English text consistent with speech at that point in history, and personal details fully supported by library research. Communications often concurrent with poltergeist-type phenomena were discovered. Webster writes a book, The Vertical Plane, with extensive photo documentation in 1989.

1985 Klaus Schreiber, West Germany, with technical assistance from Martin Wenzel, begins to get images of dead persons on TV picture tubes, using opto-electronics feedback systems. There is positive identification in many cases by accompanying audio communications, including audio-video contact with Schreiber's two deceased wives. This work is the subject of a documentary TV film and a book by Rainer Hobbe of Radio Luxembourg.

1986 Jules and Maggie Harsh-Fischbach, Luxembourg, develop and operate two electronic systems superior to that of any of the EVP equipment used up to this time.

1987 The C.E.T.L group formed, Luxembourg.

1989 Samuel Alsop publishes his book Whispers of Immortality.

1995 INIT formed (International Network for Instrumental Trans Communication, ITC)

<u>2003</u> Scottish researcher Alexander MacRae made a number of attempts to capture EVP in a specially designed laboratory belonging to the Institute of Noetic Science, Petaluma, California. The laboratory was described as being "double-screened"; Shielded against electromagnetic radiation; to prevent interference from radio transmissions or nearby electronic devices, and insulated against sound to prevent contamination of recordings by external noise sources. Over the course of the experiment, MacRae reported capturing a number of anomalies which were subsequently isolated and analyzed. Based on this analysis, and the level of screening against outside interference, MacRae concluded that the anomalies represented distinct speech from a source that could not be explained through conventional means.

EVP in the year 2007 had moved on somewhat from the image of a researcher sitting in front of a reel to reel tape recorder for hours on end waiting for a disembodied voice to break through. The digital age is upon us and technology is providing us with many more options by which to conduct our experiments. Many current researchers still prefer the use of analogue recorders to further their research, believing that the voices are imprinted on the tape electromagnetically instead of being an acoustic noise. The use of analogue recorder seems to provide us with clear voices, but not as often as we would like. The introduction of digital recorders has definitely widened our scope for research with voices being picked up far more often, but the voice quality has suffered with many of the digital voices being somewhat distorted. It is important however, to research both analogue and digital methods in the quest to advance EVP recording to new levels. Various types of microphones can be used when researching both analogue and digital methods with particular emphasis on low frequency microphones. EVP is believed to be occurring at very low frequencies, in the levels of infrasound, well below that of which the human ear is capable of hearing.

To date, EVP experiments the world over have produced far more evidence of an afterlife than any other aspect of paranormal research, or investigations.

At the present time there are thousands of individuals and organizations from all over the world actively engaged in their own EVP research. Hopefully in time through the efforts of these groups and individuals we can truly make that earth shattering all important "breakthrough", to finally make EVP a topic to be taken seriously by the masses.

Most explanations of EVP can be divided as either paranormal, explaining the source of the voice, or non-paranormal. Explanations of the non-paranormal kind usually reveal (except in the case of hoaxes) that there is actually no 'voice' at all, merely the illusion of a voice due to various effects.

A number of paranormal explanations have been suggested for the origin of EVP. Common explanations include living humans imprinting thoughts directly on an electronic medium through Psychokinesis and communication by discarnate entities such as spirits, nature energies, beings from other dimensions, or extraterrestrials.

There are a number of simple scientific explanations that can account for why some listeners to the static on audio devices may believe they hear voices including FM two way radio interference, cell phone and CB radio, baby monitors, two way voice communications through cell phones, AM or FM station radio waves, corded telephone cross talk, microwave communications, high tension electrical towers and wires and the tendency of the human brain to recognize patterns in random noise that are not really there. Some recordings may be hoaxes created by frauds or pranksters. I have found this to be the case several times. A great movie to watch and learn from is White Noise, a 2005 film starring Michael Keaton, focuses exclusively on the phenomenon of EVP and Keaton's character's attempts to contact his recently deceased wife. The filmmakers assert at the end of the film that 1 in 12 EVP messages received is threatening in nature, a figure disputed by many researchers in this field. Dennis W. Hauck a Best Selling author of, Haunted Places: The National Directory, International Directory of Haunted Places, William Shatner: a Bio-Bibliography, Captain Quirk: The Unauthorized Biography of William Shatner, is interviewed at the end of the film, and has helped me remarkably in my research and taking me further into my studies, more than he knows.

There are way too many books and magazines to list here, but most of what I found at libraries and book stores became an asset to use in my research. Following the links attached to many of the informational pages on the internet gave me plenty to digest on the topic of EVP and paranormal investigation. Simply browse all of the links you find that coincide with what you're researching and you will find a complete big picture, many avenues and paths to follow and eventually you will find the course of action that suits you best. Read all you find and send emails to anybody that is knowledgeable asking all the questions you need answers to. I found that many of the contacts were more than willing to reach out to you if they deem you serious enough, and answer any if not all your questions. Most researchers are very passionate about their work and are glad to see you take an interest.

It might take a few days for you to get a response from people over the internet, but it is well worth the wait. After getting my basic questions and facts answered, I found a snowball effect was beginning to emerge. The more basic questions I asked and got answers for, the more questions that would arise. And it seemed to be more intricate and detailed questions I started wondering about, then asking everybody. I got some great answers and I met some wonderful people and made new friends along the way. I realize we take the internet for granted now a day, but it is a wonderful tool for any study group, investigator or researcher to use to get help and answers.

There is virtually nothing in life or no topic that you can think about, that you can't get a website for, an answer to or a video explaining what you need. Not only are the methods of collecting evidence varied and complex, the equipment is even worse.

Some people were telling me I needed a Franks Ghost box, spirit communicator, spirit box, get and old broken Radio Shack AM FM radio to convert in to a communicator, an Ovilus communicator, analog vs. digital recorders, omni directional microphones, directional microphones, parabolic microphone, to go wireless or not, to use background white noise, pink noise, brown noise, or crowd noise in reverse, and the list goes on. Your head will swim to explore all the avenues available out there to capture electronic voice phenomenon, besides I would go broke in a heartbeat making all these purchases and trying to figure out what will work for me. Why, there is even a guy on the internet that for 40 bucks will convert your PC into a talking spirit box. Ok. I must admit I didn't believe I would try this one, but I did try all the rest. And I hope this book will help you get some direction and help in the way you want to start your research in the world of EVP.

You can get great results and quickly by cutting out the middle man and falling into your own category or method that works for you and sticking to it, making it a daily routine, and getting voices that will make the sample ones you here over T.V. and the internet a belly laughing joke. EVP files that will make your skin crawl, authentic communication with the dead, intelligent answers from beyond, and won't even keep you wondering what was said. I tell you, just listen to some of the so-called EVP captured on these websites and you can get some soda and popcorn and have a field day trying to guess what the beeps and whirs you will hear are saying. I personally don't believe that most of the stuff your hearing is an EVP at all, now that I have caught my own in crystal clarity voices from the dead, I think your hearing some kind of high frequency sound wave coming from some far off commercial equipment, or factory, or perhaps since most the investigators use wireless microphones and cameras, they are picking up mysterious noises coming from telephone crosstalk, or CB radios.

Why doesn't some great scientist use the best methods instead of the lame stuff that has been used up till now? Amateur and Professional musicians know that if you use inferior sound equipment, you will produce a wreck for a recording or performance. So it would seem to me that a 29 dollar radio with a bent pin would not work as well for a team or researchers like that of the best equipment would. And remember I think that the more knowledge you have, and quality equipment you use, and to keep to a routine using it all, would give you an advantage to get the best results you have ever heard. I think I had listened to over 5000 EVPs from various groups some of them were just astounding, and others were just hysterical. I thought to myself many times, if I only had swamp land in Florida, I could make a mint from these people. It was uncanny the sentences they claim they hear and can make out completely from these buzzes, whirs and scrapes.

Ok. Enough bashing the groups and societies that are just grandstanding for web time, I really do want you to look at some of this stuff, just to get in the right mind set, and know that you can get much clearer, class A, (I will go into the classifications later on in this book), pertinent conversation with intelligent spirits captured on sound files by listening to all the methods out there and reading my book, and taking all the information and finding the most natural way for you to achieve direct communication with the dead. What works for others will not work for you, trust me, I found that out after spending a lot of money and time. I have now a rigid method I follow every day at approximately the same time, and it works spectacularly. I will coach you on equipment, time of day, dialog and methods later on in this book. I will try to leave no stone unturned for you. It is much easier than trying all of the applications I just mentioned on your own.

And one other thing, if you try this research and get a spirit answering your questions and you freak out, then this research is not for you. You must be well grounded, in charge and be empowered by the fact that you know the spirits cannot and will not harm you. This is not Hollywood, they will not drag you across the bed at night, fling you out of a window, or stab you with flying knives. I have stated this so many times to so many people I have come in contact with and I still believe it today, if spirits could harm people, then why after 2740 people lost their lives on 911, is Ben Laden still alive? Can't harm you, and will not harm you, because these spirits were once just like you and I, families, a home, a car, a job and these shows that start their EVP sessions by screaming at a spirit "come out, show yourself, right now!!", is ridiculous. If I were dead, I wouldn't answer them at all talking to me that way, but that is just me. Take this time to think about that, think if you were a spirit, how would you react to provoking, and ordering you around. I think deep down inside these investigators don't really want an answer, they want the spirit to clam up because they don't know how to deal with one when it does say something. Of course it is just my opinion, but like I said, if I were a spirit I would want to talk to the person trying to communicate with me who is compassionate, loving, and caring about me and my situation, and who wants to help me get my message across, not some tyrant ordering me around.

Speaking of message, most of the spirits around you are just trying to give you one, letting you know that they are here and around you all the time. They are loved ones, friends and neighbors, and again, this is 95% of the time. Your family will keep giving you messages until you get it, coins on the floor, objects moved about, knocking or rapping on stuff in and around the house. They are not trying to scare you; they are trying to communicate with you the best way they know how. This is a very cool thing to have happen, and I have found once you get the hint, they stop doing it.

Say like, "OK Aunt Betty, I know you are here, I love it, you keep watch over us, it is ok to be here with us, but just don't freak us out, we love you and make sure you don't show yourself to the kids, they will have issues the rest of their life." And every now and again, when you're alone, talk to Aunt Betty, tell her you love her, and you appreciate the fact that she is watching over you, it makes you feel special and loved. And always ask permission to record their voice, or take photographs in advance, it is only proper and gives them a heads up.

So what are EVP's, or Electronic Voice Phenomena? They are thought to be many things. No one really knows for certain, as with so many other aspects of the paranormal field. One thing is for sure though, that true EVP's are based on frequency, not on how good they sound. Don't get me wrong, clear, and precise is great, and that is what we strive for, but the frequency is very important. Some EVP's are recorded at less than 300 Hertz with a few going as low as 80Hz. And at the other end of the spectrum, they have been recorded above 20,000 Hz and could be over as much as 22,000Hz.

Ok, on to classifications. EVP's are thought to have four categories or classifications, A, B, C, and R with the class A being the absolute best. It is very audible and clear to the human ear. Anyone listening to a class A recording will be able to tell exactly what is said, and so will anybody else in the room. A class B recording is still very audible, but not very clear or distinct in the formation of words. They need to be listened to over and over in order to understand what was said. You can use a noise reducer in an attempt to clear up the message, but it will still be hard to find out what has been expressed. A class C recording is not good at all. It could be as low as a whisper, or it could have been software and /or a microphone problem. Never the less, you cannot make out what is being said and it sounds just like a glitch or scratch on a record, and could be so faint you may not catch it the first or second time around.

A class R recording is a regular class A, B, or C EVP but with a twist, it is almost like a mirror effect that occurs in that a different message or meaning will become apparent if the captured voice or sound is reversed. Because of this factor, I feel that all captured EVP's should be listened to in reverse to make sure that this has not happened. You could have two completely different messages occupying the same space. If the voice or sound makes more sense in reverse that when it is played forward, or if it has any meaning to it at all when played in reverse, then I would classify it as an R.

So the main disagreement about EVP's being paranormal in nature and not radio waves or human voices is blown out of the water by their frequency, not there clarity or quality. There is no way a living human person could speak or form words in frequencies under 300 Hertz or over 20,000 Hertz.

True EVP's are classified under 300Hz or above 20,000Hz

Human Voice (able to form words) is 300hz up to 3.500Hz

Human Hearing 20Hz up to 20,000Hz

AM radio waves range from 535.000Hz up to 1,705,000Hz

FM radio waves range from 88,000,000Hz up to 108,000,000Hz

Microwave communication (not your oven) from 2.0 to 44.0 GHz

Cordless Phone range is 40,000,000 up to 50,000,000Hz

Cell Phone range is 824,000,000Hz up to 849,000,000Hz

Alarm system and garage door range is around 40,000,000Hz

Baby monitors operate at 49,000,000Hz

This confusing frequency part is why I use only wired microphones and not wireless audio. I realize that you could still get crosstalk over shielded microphone cables, but the possibilities are rather remote that you will get "breaker, breaker one nine, making a pit stop," over a hard wired audio microphone, or a crying baby at a neighbor's house needing changed confused with an actual recorded EVP.

Further Reading & Research Material

✓ Breakthrough: An Amazing Experiment in Electronic Communication with the Dead

By Konstantin Raudive (1971)

This book is the documented result of a 'six year' arduous research into an astounding scientific phenomenon, accidentally discovered in Sweden by Friedrich Jürgenson in 1957. 'Breakthrough' was the catalyst for many of today's EVP researchers.

✓ The Ghost of 29 Megacycles

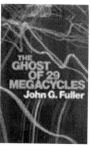

By John G Fuller (1985)

Is it possible that, when certain audio frequencies are combined with a tape recorder, the dead can communicate with us, not through a medium but using their own voices? If the phenomenon could be proved beyond doubt, the implications were enormous: it could be the biggest break-through in the history of mankind.

✓ Phone Calls from the Dead

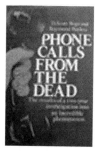

By D Scott Rogo & Raymond Bayless (1979)

In 1968, Mrs. Don Owens of Ohio received an urgent call for help from a friend. The time of the call was 10:30 p.m, the exact time he was pronounced dead at a local hospital. Two parapsychologists undertook and intense two-year investigation into this puzzling phenomenon. Rogo and Bayless conclude that these enigmatic phone calls actually do occur.

Carry On Talking (UK)/Voices from the Tapes (US),

By Peter Bander (1973)

Few discoveries have caused a greater controversy then the Voice phenomenon of Raudive and Jurgenson. Are they really the voices of people whom we know to be dead? Leading electronics engineers, physicists, and psychologists carried out controlled experiments…and over 200 messages came through. Peter Bander tells his amazing story.

Roads to Eternity

By Sarah Estep (2005)

EVP, Electronic Voice Phenomena, is real. Spirits can communicate with us from beyond the grave and author Sarah Estep has the proof. She has had more than 20,000 contacts with the spirit world, and has caught EVP on tape recorders, her computer, her TV, and even her telephone. Hear it for yourself on the Roads to Eternity bonus CD included with the book.

Voices of Eternity

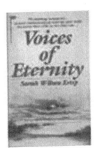

By Sarah Estep (1988)

"This is a book that everyone interested in the possibility of communicating with a departed loved one will want to read." says Harold Sherman, from the foreword of Voices of Eternity. This book can be downloaded in PDF format from the American Association of Electronic Voice Phenomena which was founded by Sarah Estep.

Voices of the Dead

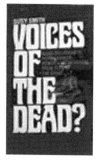

By Susy Smith (1977)

Are the mysterious speakers recorded on tape really present though invisible to the Living? Spirit voices have been are even now reaching out across the barrier of death to communicate with the living … Countless people have explored and tested this phenomenon, and psychic Susy Smith presents their extraordinary experience.

Talks with the Dead

By William Adams Welch (1975)

"That night I heard my first spirit voice on the tapes. With an exquisite sense of the apropos, it said, 'Hello.'" With this experience William Welch began the painstaking but thrilling research which led to the breakthroughs he now shares …His experiments with taped voices present new evidence that man can have intelligible communications with the dead…that, in fact, there is life after death.

EVP and New Dimensions

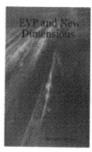

Alexander Macrae 2004

This must be the most comprehensive and up-to-date book on the Electronic Voice Phenomenon (EVP). Written by a former NASA speech researcher, the book covers everything from basic questions, such as what is EVP, how it is done, to a wide-ranging discussion of new dimensions.

The Scole Experiment

By Grant & Jane Solomon (1999)

This book is the extraordinary results of a five year investigation into life after death. In 1993, four psychic researchers embarked on a series of experiments in the Norfolk village of Scole. The subsequent events were so astounding that senior members of the prestigious Society for Psychical Research asked to observe, test, and record what took place.

There Is No Death and There Are No Dead

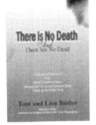

By Tom & Lisa Butler (2003)

Anyone interested in communication with a departed loved one or learning more about the "Other Side" will want to read this book. Many people may be shocked to learn that the so called dead have been communicating across the veil through electronic devices since the early 1900s.

Other recommended books include - The Vertical Plane written By Ken Webster, Whispers of Immortality written By Samuel Alsop,

Chapter Two:

Confusion & Contradictions

Alright, now that we have read all the research, books, magazines, and website knowledge that we can stand, now what? As you may have noticed, (how could you not), there are lot of methods and tricks of the trade tips on how to be successful at capturing EVP's. The majority of them contradict each other, in a lot of areas, from which equipment to use, provoke or be nice, do I wait 15 seconds or a full minute between questions? And let's see, should I use white noise, pink noise, brown noise, market day crowd noise played in reverse, or should I tune in the radio to an empty station, or maybe the T.V. to a blank channel? Some of the information I got even wanted me to use, and showed me plans to build a Jacob's ladder to produce electricity and waft ozone in to the room to heighten the energy levels before I conducted my session of EVP recording. And then there is the monster of a question, what time of day? Wow! They even have lunar time tables with charts and graphs, and sun spot events all mapped out for you in calendar form for the next few years. I got to the point where I was discouraged and thought I don't want to chart planets, or become an astrologer, I just want to record some EVP's from the comfort of my home. And I might add here, absolutely nobody could tell me how loud the background noises should be while recording. They all said, just whatever works for you. Well, that was the best thing I had heard yet. Whatever works for me!

That is when I decided to try a few experiments on my own armed with the knowledge I attained in my intense research mode, and just do it. It had become very apparent that there is no wrong way if you have the basic principles down to a science.

With an outline of what I wanted to accomplish in my tests and trial experiments, I pushed onward and upward knowing that I could do this over and over until I came up with a routine that worked for me. Well, I took a deep breath and jotted down an opening statement and some general questions, and I started to feel a little like Thomas A. Edison when he came up with these very pertinent really great quotes:

"Results! Why, man, I have gotten a lot of results, I know several things that won't work."

"Hell, there are no rules here – We're trying to accomplish something."

"I am not discouraged, because every wrong attempt discarded, is another step forward."

"Our greatest weakness lies in giving up. The most certain way to succeed is always to try just one more time."

Man, he was so right! I began recording my own voice with an opening statement, and around 20 questions leaving about 15 seconds between each. After I played it back, I adjusted the levels of the input volume watching the VU meter constantly on the recorder. I didn't want to over modulate, I wanted it to be crystal clear enough to hear any and all responses no matter how trivial. Then, I added some white noise and recorded it all over again, using the same methodical way, and played it back adjusting the background noise volume level to suit me. Like I said, nobody was very sure how loud or soft it should be, just that it be in the background. I recorded and played back about 40 times using different settings and kept a written log, or journal of each attempt, noting the exact levels of everything including how far away from the microphone I was. I also was mindful that most researchers do agree that as soon as you press the record button, give a little air time before you start in with your dialog as this is prime time for something to be caught on tape.

After I got the hang of the equipment, I then turned to the type of background noise, be it white, pink, brown or crowd. I tried them all one at a time again and again till I felt the levels of both my voice and the noise didn't conflict with each other. I have no idea to this day if the backgrounds were too loud or soft, it just felt natural to me. I entered in to my journal, the moon phases and sunspot data for a while, but in the end, I personally found that I could get great recordings no matter what was going on in the atmosphere, or stratosphere. One thing I agree on with most of the other researcher's, is a routine. A set schedule of the same time every day netted me the best results.

Still trying to utilize all of the tried and true methods everybody else was using, alternating them from day to day and logging the results eventually brought me to a method that ended up being the best for me.

Now time of day was a big contradiction among other teams as well, some say "no matter what time of day," others say "wee hours of the morning, around 3am is best." So once again it is trial and error time with different hours of the day and night. A bunch of EVP teams conveyed to me that three to four days before and after a full moon is outrageously the max time period. But, again nobody could come up with an approximate hour, so I tried all hours of the day, each and every hour on the hour for the full four days before, during and after the full moon phase, and every half hour when it came to the blue moon week. Of course make sure you log every time, with or without results. And to be perfectly honest, I never got squat for over 61 sessions in a row. Not a peep, not even one of those buzz, or whir noises, the big goose egg. Natta!

I figured I was simply doing it wrong and needed to rethink my strategy. Maybe increase or change the background noise, or even get rid of it all together, or could it be the questions I was asking. I really didn't want to provoke the spirits into communicating because that is just not my style. I rewrote the questions and revised the opening statement, being mindful of not changing too much at once, so I wouldn't confuse myself and left the background noise alone for now. Another 30 sessions came and went with not a response in the bunch, I even started to look into the television method of images and responses, but that seemed really confusing, like what channel to turn to, and if you do try this experiment, make sure you turn off the blue screen feature on the DVR, or VCR to let the noise signal come through, I've been told. (Oops). I never really gave this the good old college try, but perhaps I will in the near future. Right now though, I am very satisfied with the results I am getting by sticking to a routine, first meditation, then my opening statement that is geared toward inviting anyone to communicate with me, then asking my 20 general questions, and finally closing the door and ending the session. I found that this regimen works really great for me and I have continued this practice to this day.

Always be aware of your background surroundings while you record your sessions, such as birds, neighbors going to work, the mail man, trash pickup, surface road traffic and highway sounds if you live close to one and of course your telephone. If you happen to live in an apartment or townhouse complex, sounds of people living everyday life next door could be a problem like music, television and radios, climbing up the stairs and the occasional laughing or argument right in the middle of your recording. I have had friends and relatives sit in on recording sessions from time to time, and I have instructed them to be as quiet as they can be. Tag or make an audible notation during your recording if a normal everyday sound interrupts your experiment. I have often stated a tag like, "ok...that was my pen I dropped right here," or "that was me coughing and clearing my throat just now." It just helps you later when you try to analyze the results so there can be no mistake with the unfamiliar noise you have found.

I want to mention now that I have also found a few researchers that do not agree with the use of background noise during recording because they feel that just like our imagination can make any shape out of clouds in the sky, we can manufacture in our minds any false EVP result within the constant fluctuations of the noise patterns. Our minds will tell us that we have heard something that is not really there, and therefore the noise is more of a hindrance than a help. I tried all of the background noises in my experiments, but really didn't get much of a result.

To make a short conclusion, at least what I discovered in my trials, is that for the most part they are right. I found that I had to listen even more carefully during the playback and had to repeat over and over a segment to discern if there really was something on the recording or if my mind just thought there was something notable. For me, I don't use background noise anymore and have abandoned any research experiment utilizing its properties. The equipment I use supplies me with all of the noise or hiss from frequency and surroundings I need, so I rely strictly on what is natural now. I simply chose a normally quiet time of the day, light a candle, turn on the recorder and begin my general question plan of attack. By the way, if I do get an intelligent EVP that is blatantly answering my general questions or declaring a name perhaps, I will tailor my next session to include questions specifically directed to that spirit to which I have communicated with previously, calling them by name and attempting to get them to respond to me once more. This has happened successfully many times. Make sure that on the next session you use a specific dialog geared toward the comments and answers you received on your previous encounter with the intelligent spirit. Attempt to get more in-depth with your questions, assessing what the spirit wants or needs. Remember, the answers to your questions can only be heard during playback of the session, so any additional information you can obtain will be helpful in continuing future discovery type conversations.

You can realistically maintain a relationship with a spirit for a long time, but keep in mind they need to find and enter the light, so please help them.

Analog Recorders

Up until the late 90's, analog recorders were the only means of capturing EVP available to researchers. From early reel to reel recorders to solid state professional audio recorders, there are many variations available to you on the market today. It traditionally takes longer to capture EVP on an analog recorder, but when you do, you will find that the voices are much clearer than that of digital with a higher capture rate of class "A" disembodied voices. Many of today's researchers still prefer the use of analog recorders during their experiments due to the clarity of the voices coming through. You will find that analog recordings contain a high level of background hiss, which is where many of the disembodied voices can be found during analysis, thus for me, eliminating the need for any outside, or manufactured background noise. I recommend the use of an external mic which should be positioned a few feet from the recorder to avoid the noisy mechanism of the recorder contaminating your final recordings. Many experimenters do not believe in the use of the portable cassette recorders, but they work for me as long as you keep the units motor noise away from the microphone, although I do not use them on a regular basis. Always use a fresh cassette tape when starting a new recording session as tapes can get worn over time. Previous recordings may not be overwritten, or erased properly and may bleed through the tape onto newer recordings and give you false EVP evidence or at the very least, not a clear recording. Many researchers will have completely different takes on this subject, again whatever makes you more comfortable with your experiments. This is your show and your money, only you know what you can afford and/or are willing to spend.

Digital Recorders

The digital age is upon us and there are many digital audio recorders available on the market, from basic digital Dictaphones to solid state professional digital audio recorders. Digital recorders are extremely portable and most have an in built microphone. Many of them have a built in flash memory that can give you hours of recording at the touch of a button and files can be managed easily. Some have found that digital recorders are most effective for capturing EVP when used on the lowest quality settings which creates another topic for debate. These settings appear to generate a higher degree of background hiss which is where many of the voices it is perceived can be found. This is much like using white noise as carrier signal for EVP voices to come through.

One of the most talked about digital recorders for recording EVP is that of the Panasonic RR-DR60 IC Recorder. The RR-DR60 is a voice activated recorder that has shown over time that it is highly effective for capturing EVP. I found that the voice activated part of the recorder didn't always work for some of the lower volume voices and could even be missing some. Inexplicable voices seem to come through on this recorder in abundance, even when used inside a Faraday Cage to rule out external interference. Unfortunately many of voices captured on the RR-DR60 seem to be extremely distorted and require much work using filtering software. None the less, these recorders are extremely interesting from a research point of view and many more experiments are required to find out why this recorder is so effective in comparison to other digital recorders. Unfortunately the Panasonic RR-DR60 is hard to come by these days. The Sony ICD range of recorders are also highly effective for capturing EVP and like many other digital recorders, can be slipped into your pocket and taken just about anywhere for experimentation purposes. I recommend experimenting with many different digital recorders and comparing the results.

External Microphones

External microphones can be used with any recording device that has an input socket for its use. I utilize many different microphones during experimentation including parabolic microphones. Induction microphones, condenser microphones, dynamic microphones and radio microphones (wireless). I tend to stay away from wireless because during my trials and experiments, crosstalk and interference from all of the other gadgets the world has to offer was coming through like gang busters. It is important to experiment with different types of microphone during research as they can all have their own distinctive sound. Choose the method that works the best for your location and one that is complementary to your experiments. Two of the most useful microphones are the parabolic which is used to pick up distant noise and amplify noise that occurs in close proximity, and the omni-directional mic. I mainly experiment with different microphones using an analog recorder.

Desktop/Laptop Computers

It is possible to record sound directly onto a laptop or desktop computer via an attached microphone. Many researchers use this method and have successfully captured many EVP voices recording directly using software such as Voyetra Audio Surgeon or Adobe Audition. Of course, computers are essential for analyzing your recordings and laptops in particular are excellent for field recording. If your laptop or desktop computer has record direct to disk this feature would be preferred because it is better than recording to your hard drive in the remote likely hood of a power outage at least some of your recordings could be saved.

Inter Frequency

The Inter Frequency method of EVP recording is used by many of today's researchers and was also a favorite of past researchers such as Friedrich

Jurgenson, Konstantin Raudive and Raymond Cass. This method involves providing a background carrier noise while recording, such as white noise which was traditionally provided by tuning a radio in between channels. Many skeptics believe that the anomalous voices picked up in this way are actually stray radio signals. Interestingly enough we have never come across any cases where music has been recorded using this method, which is the main content of today's radio broadcasts, but again, you be the judge. You can generate various frequency tones for experimentation purposes such as white noise, pink noise and brown noise or crowd background or reverse crowd background using software such as Audio Surgeon or Adobe Audition to avoid the need for a radio. I recommend experimenting with various different frequency tones during research. Some researchers have even suggested using the relaxation therapy sound machines set on water running, or one of those small desktop relaxing water features.

Raudive Diode

Konstantin Raudive devised his own method of improving the quality of his EVP recordings. Through experimentation he found that using a Germanium Diode plugged into a recorder instead of a microphone vastly helped improve the quality of the voices. I have found that the Germanium Diode is capable of picking up radio waves and is best utilized in conjunction with a Faraday Cage (see below). You will find that the diode will not pick up your own voice or any noise contamination from your recording area. I highly recommend experimenting with this device if you can get a hold of one.

Faraday Cage

The Faraday Cage is a very useful tool for EVP research. The cage is utilized to shield your recording equipment and to effectively wipe out the chances of electromagnetic or radio interference coming through on your recordings. A very good example of a Faraday Cage is the cooking compartment of a microwave oven which is designed to stop microwaves escaping, thus eliminating any chance of over exposure. Try placing your mobile cell phone inside an unplugged microwave and calling it from a land line. You will find that the signal will not get through. Utilizing a microwave for home EVP experiments is an ideal way to ensure that your EVP voices cannot be explained by electromagnetic or radio interference. Try this little experiment, it works.

Telephones & Answering Machines

There are many reported cases around the world of EVP or anomalous voices appearing on telephone answering machines, even in the modern age of digital telephone exchanges where crossed lines are virtually impossible. There are also many cases of people having telephone conversation with friends or family members who have long since departed this world. I have had experience with this and I am truly fascinated by these other cases. I would very much like to hear from anyone who has experienced anomalous voices via the telephone to further my research in this area. When listening to telephone answering machine messages always pay particular attention to the start, and the end for voices breaking through. This phenomenon seems to occur on both digital and analog answering machines and there have even been cases of mobile cell phone messages containing anomalous voices.

I have provided some basic information about EVP recording equipment and recording techniques. Of course there are many more methods of recording EVP and I recommend experimenting with as many methods as your time and funds will allow. There is so much to learn about the reasons why these voices appear on our recording equipment, so please do not be scared to try something new. The next breakthrough could be just around the corner, and you could be the one to discover it!

Chapter Three: 3

The Game Plan

It's time to decide which direction you want to take, record EVP's in the field, in the studio, or like me, both. I really started out in the field first recording with just a $50 dollar hand held digital recorder, and then graduated to integrate the studio quality method into our investigations. I eventually incorporated the studio method with my team's investigations about two years ago. With a total of 6 high quality omni-directional microphones, 1200 feet of cable connected to a rack mounted 12 channel mixing board which is then patched into a dual deck analog cassette recorder, I can change the whole investigative area into a fully covered sound stage. I can hear a pin drop in the area that is being investigated by just turning on the power in the room where the team member is conducting his or her EVP session, or turn them all on and make the complete venue come alive, nothing, not one sound will go unrecorded. The quality of recording you can get no matter what class it is, is astounding, the investigators still carry the hand held digital recorders which we use as a backup source and personal diary. If you can't hear something very clearly from the main recording, you always have use of the individual's digital recording for further review.

I think it is a great time to tell you that if you are getting into the paranormal fields, no matter which path you choose, for monetary gain, think again, there is no money in it. Actually it is more of a drain on your wallet than you may think. Working at a fast food restaurant would be a step up on the money train for you rather than this research topic. The investigations in private homes and businesses are no charge projects. I know that some groups charge a nominal fee, but most of the passionate serious ones do not.

Even the sensitive I frequently use feels that his talent is a gift from God and he should never profit from it. It is to help his fellow man and help cross wayward or lost souls into the light. He assured me that he has never and will never charge for his services in these instances. Now for you gifted psychic people out there, I realize that you may charge for a personal one on one reading or connection and that is ok, but for helping the police find a lost loved one or in solving a crime, it's your call if you want to charge or not.

The main difference between field work and lab experiments is the equipment needed. I will go into this more intensely in the coming chapters. If you choose to do field investigations, you will need to have pretty much every piece of equipment portable and within easy reach. A cloth nail apron for about $3 bucks from a hardware store works wonders to keep things at your side. Also take into consideration that you either have to join a paranormal group or team or start your own troop. Then you have to wait for people to contact you with their ghostly problems and that means you have to get your name out there for people to even know you exist. In today's world, there are so many skeptics you wouldn't even believe, they think even though you're not charging them one red cent, that you are still running a scam somehow.

I get at least 10 potential investigators email me per day asking if they could join our team, so I am sure it is very difficult to find one that will include you. Now with that said, there is nothing wrong with doing EVP's in a controlled environment at home while you wait for that big investigation call or acceptance letter from the team you just put in an application for. And please be careful of the groups out there that want to know up front what pieces of equipment you already own before they accept your application, they may just be looking to upgrade their gear for free instead of gaining a good investigator.

I know that I sound very negative about other paranormal groups, and there are some extremely great ones around me in Ohio. But, I have asked permission to investigate known haunted sites only to get the reply of NO! No way! When I ask why the story seems to be the exact same one I have heard time and time again, "well I let some groups in and I end up cleaning up pizza boxes and beer cans the next morning." Really, pizza and beer cans? What are these groups here for? Did they need a free place to party? I am getting really tired of the startup groups putting the nix on every legitimate group and tying our hands behind our back because they have no purpose other than to just have blowout fun. Now, I don't mean have the most serious, swat team attitude at the site, of course have fun, but pizza and beer clean up in the morning from the owner or caretaker, please! And by the way, the startup groups will never last past a year or two anyway, but the irreversible damage has already been done. There are now logging chains and pad locks on almost every Mausoleum in Ohio, yes I know, mostly due to the scrap metal thieves, but in part to keep people from destroying history, it is history by the way. I have seen the destruction of grave markers when shaving cream has been use to make out the inscriptions. Just be mindful of other people's property, have reverence for the dead, and check out a group as completely as you can before you join, don't get caught up in a destructive, just for fun past time, bring pizza and beer type group.

Ok. On the other hand, if you choose the in home paranormal EVP lab, you answer to no one, and can make trips to the fridge anytime you want. The experiments are completely your ideas, no newspaper adds to buy, no costly website hosting company to pay or pages to maintain to get a message out that your available for investigations, and no group to join. You never have to ask anybodies permission, (accept the spirits) to conduct your research. I really enjoy this angle and I have gotten some wonderful results that have just floored me, and have even stumped some University analysts.

Now on to costs, to be honest with you it has cost me about the exact amount going down either path. In the field of investigations, it is mostly hand held gadgetry that can become very expensive the more you gear up. EMF, K2, laser temps, motion detectors, portable recorders, walkie-talkies, flashlights, night vision video camcorders and surveillance cameras, tripods, monitors, DVR to record surveillance and the list goes on. For the home office or lab, you will need an analog recorder deck and 90 minute cassette tapes, killer headphones, studio quality microphone(s), and great analyzing user friendly software.

Chapter Four: 4

Essential Research Equipment

Now that we have discussed the different fields of study you may want to get into, we need to go over the absolute "must have" equipment for each of the two fields in order for you to function successfully. I have also added most of the equipment required in the field of paranormal investigation, as opposed to the in-home lab.

FIELD STUDY AND INVESTIGATIONS

Paranormal events cause energy disturbances across the entire electromagnetic spectrum (low-frequency infrared through visible light and on into high-frequency ultraviolet energy and finally x-ray and gamma rays). It seems paranormal events tap into existing energy sources around us to manifest in our reality and disrupt our natural (or background) energy levels. These unexplainable fluctuations are genuine evidence of paranormal activity. There are seven main categories of electronic detection instruments used by investigators to capture these energy fluctuations associated with paranormal phenomena. EMF Detectors, Temperature Sensors, Static Electricity & Ionization Detectors, Motion Detectors, EVP & Listening Devices, RF Detectors, and Radiation Monitors.

 Electromagnetic Field Detectors: Three kinds of instruments are generally used to detect electro-magnetic fields (EMF). They are the electric field, magnetic field, and radio frequency (RF) meters. The favorite for most paranormal researchers are the Multi-Field Meters, which measure two to three of these fields at once. They usually feature a fast reacting needle gauge, at least two sensitivity scales, and are very easy to use.

Other meters monitor the combined magnetic and electric field strength and are known as Gaussmeters or Teslameters. The ELF (Extremely Low Frequency) models are best for paranormal research. For monitoring microwave and radio frequencies and can also help detect hidden sound or spy equipment, the paranormal researchers make use of RF Meters. It should be noted that all gauss meters, electric field meters, RF/microwave meters, etc. can only measure the strength of the field at the location of the meter. The meters can be placed in stationary positions or used like mobile probes while walking around during an investigation. What distinguishes one meter from another is the sensitivity (or the smallest field strength that the meter can detect). For instance, a gauss meter with sensitivity of 0.1 mG (milligauss) is ten times more sensitive than a meter that can only detect down to 1.0 mG. While a more sensitive meter can be successfully used further away from the source of the field, it is still only measuring the weaker field at the location of the meter. In looking for a more sensitive meter, compare the minimum sensitivity rating of one meter to another. How effectively a meter can detect a field depends on the strength of the field at the source, the pattern of radiation from the source, and the rate that the field decreases with distance ($1/d$, $1/d^2$, $1/d^3$, etc.). Some EMF sources may have symmetrical field patterns, some may not. A single-axis detector is sensitive to the field directly in front of the probe and must be rotated during use to find the proper orientation to the source field being measured to get accurate readings, while a three-axis detector is sensitive all around the probe and is omni-directional which means it takes readings at all angles without being moved about. Price range $30 to $200.

Temperature Sensors will single out cold spots which is a depletion of energy caused by paranormal events. Cold spots seem to be short lived and move around a lot, conventional thermometers are not equipped to handle the fast paced changes in readings so the pistol type laser device is best suited here.

The accepted way to check for cold spots is instant-reading infrared digital thermometers. It is best to add a laser pointer to these meters for good aim, in which case all that the investigator has to do is point and shoot to get instant temperature readings of surfaces 10 to 50 or more feet away. For ambient or background temperature readings, a common thermometer or thermocouple device is sufficient. Price range $50 to $200.

Static Electricity & Ionization Detectors: Paranormal activity can ionize the air to produce negatively charged particles called ions. This phenomenon is easy to measure with an air ion counter. Static electricity and ionization emit light when the source field discharges into the air. Also, high ionization levels sometimes indicate the presence of radioactivity, and a Geiger counter survey might be indicated in this case. Price range $500 to $800.

EVP & Listening Devices make it possible to actually listen to EMF energy levels and patterns, and sometimes this proves a very effective means of investigation of paranormal events. Although it is less quantitative, it provides immediate and very personal feedback. Electronic Voice Phenomena (EVP) has been picked up on just about any common recording devices from radios and tape recorders to televisions. For field paranormal research, the best tool is a hand held digital recorder that can be uploaded directly into a personal computer for analysis. Remember, some investigators swear by the cheap models because of the presence of static or hiss which can be used by spirit to form words. Price range $30 to $200.

RF Detectors are Radio frequency meters that measure in the general range of 1-4500 MHz (or 4.5 GHz). This is a range of the electromagnetic spectrum used for communications and the devices can be used to check for cell phone activity, concealed bugging devices, remote cameras, etc. Sometimes paranormal phenomena have been associated with the lower range of RF signals as well as short bursts of high energy microwaves. It is known that human cells generate low RF frequencies, although there is no proven scientific explanation for why this occurs. Price range $180 to $300.

Radiation Monitors: Radioactive objects sometimes emit a greenish light as well as scintillating white sparks (visible only in complete darkness) and more than once have been responsible for alleged "hauntings." On the other hand, spontaneous radioactive events have been associated with genuine anomalous activity of all sorts. Researchers have found that fluctuations in background radiation can indicate a disturbance in spirit energy. Price range $300 to $500.

Digital or Analog Sound Level Meter: This device allows you to measure the intensity of sounds from any source. High spikes on the meter, yet you can't hear it is congruent with spirit activity. Price range $50 to $200.

Night Vision Camcorders: You should want a night vision camcorder to record paranormal events in the field. Most models are equipped with sound and they can be used as irrefutable backup evidence when it comes to EVP's. I really don't like the DVD disk ones (at least the ones I have used), you catch a lot of the spinning disk noise while you're recording, makes catching EVP's quite a bit harder. You may want to include an additional battery powered Infrared light source as the built in light is dim. Price range $300 to $900.

Digital Camera: Somewhere along the line you will want a digital camera, up to 10 megapixels is about average, just make sure it can take rapid fire pictures and can hold high speed, high capacity digital media cards. A four gig digital card will hold about 2000 pictures at 10 megapixels. Now I realize the little cameras are cheaper, but this camera can be had with a 24x zoom, face detection and more for under $300. You will want a neck strap, the little wrist straps are a pain in the butt, and end up in the way of the shot almost every time.

In summary you need to purchase at the very least a medium quality ($30) to high quality ($100) digital hand held recorder if you are going just for EVP's. Preferably a recorder with separate numbered files I find is the best one to have, it is easier to keep track of which area you recorded in while separating sessions for non-confusing replay, as long as you time and date tag at the beginning and end of each session. Tagging is the most important procedure you can do to remedy confusion and false evidence spots on your playback. If you hear an unfamiliar noise and think, wow I got one, and then the investigator says, "I just opened the door to the basement", you know what is going on. If nobody says a word about what action or actions they took while the session was in progress, you will be analyzing the recording for an hour trying to put things in perspective before you finally throw out the evidence or give up trying to figure what was going on.

IN HOME EVP RESEARCH LAB

 Cassette Dual Deck Recorder: You need to have either an analog cassette tape deck or connect your studio quality microphone to your computer for a direct recording input.

Again, I record to this machine and download to my computer only if evidence is found. When purchasing the deck, make sure it has an output for stereo headphones. Most dual decks offered by several companies range in price from $150 to $300, and good quality used units sell on e-bay from $50 to 100, however, watch for outrageous shipping charges.

Studio Quality Microphone: There are many brands of excellent studio quality omni-directional microphones on the market. Make sure you get omni-directional which in short means it will pick up in a 360° radius and cover the entire office or lab. You only need one for the lab, but may want at least 4 to 6 for field research. Most of these units do not come with the cable to connect to your computer or sound mixing board so make sure you choose which way you're going to use it before you purchase the wires. They even make USB models which might work great for your home lab. I use only desktop adjustable mic stands, that expand up to about 24 inches off the ground and of course each one is in a shock mount bracket to eliminate floor vibration when walking past. Microphones range in price from $50 to $300 each, the desktop adjustable stands were about $15 each.

 Mixing Board: Now these were my personal preferences when it came to a sound mixing board. It had to have at least 12 channels, rack mounted in a mobile case to make it portable, (you can skip this feature if you're not going to put it to use in the field and go for a mixing console instead), it had to have phantom power because most of the quality microphones require phantom power to work, must be stereo and most of all it had to be inexpensive. It gave me the option to turn on or off each microphone in different locations, adjust the level of sound for each, and also came with an external headphone jack and recorder output jacks in the rear. Price range is $150 to $1000.

 Over The Ear Headphones: Do not skimp on the headphones! This can end up being your weakest link in the system if you let it be. Most models over $100, will be fine but keep in mind, this is what you will use every day in the field or lab, to listen to your possible evidence. You can't catch a thing if you can't hear it. Also, there are ear buds that sound really good, but I feel that these are personal items and I don't want to share a personal item that someone puts in their ears. That's just me. One note, make sure in the lab when you start recording an EVP session, the headphones go in the recorder phone jack, not the mixing board output phone jack. This is a tip I got from experience in the field. I still remember it like it was yesterday the sound was phenomenal, I could hear a pin drop through the headphones, the fact is the recording level on the dual deck was at a minimum and the first whole 90 minutes of recording was junk. I could hear it, but the recorder couldn't. This is just food for thought. Price range $19 to $500 and any dollar amount you can afford in between.

In a nut shell, you can spend as little or as much as you can afford on this research project. The main factor in all this depends on which way you're headed when it comes to what you want to do. Field research is not for everybody, some investigators find that working with people in their homes is not for them, and sitting in a lab, day after day talking into a microphone basically saying the same thing over and over, hoping to catch the golden grail of EVP is not for everybody either. I will say that it works either way you choose, and I am still amazed at the results I personally have captured. The addition of the studio quality sound equipment to our field excursions has yielded humongous evidence for us. I have had to put little snap and glow lights on the microphones to keep investigators from tripping and falling over them, not the big .99¢ a piece ones, the little glowing green fishing bobber ones about 1 inch long and ¼ inch wide. Make sure you purchase the proper wires and cables to hook up your equipment, before you get in the field. Always test it at home for an evening if it is field equipment before you get to the clients site. Take at least 6 blank cassette tapes and 6 VCR or DVD blank tapes and media. It is very hard to find an open store in a remote part of the country at 3am to find patch cords, extra batteries and DVD disks or blank tapes.

This is my EVP lab equipment setup

Top....A small 7" television monitor

Next...larger 12" surveillance monitor

Next...A graphic sound equalizer

Next...Two VCR-DVR combo decks

Next...A 12 channel sound mixing board

Next...A dual analog cassette recorder

Bottom...Two dual GO.VIDEO editors

The mobile cases I made out of ¾ inch plywood panels then covered them with black automotive carpet and put heavy duty handles on either side to carry to the site.

As I stated, I use this equipment in our field investigations and connect 6 night vision cameras to record video and 6 omni-directional phantom powered microphones to record EVP's. The dual analog cassette recording deck is great because I can leave the unit run and it will automatically record on side A then switch to side B on the first tape, then convert to side A and switch to side B on the second tape continuously. I only have to change the two cassette tapes every 180 minutes and get full coverage of the entire investigative area. The same goes for the night vision cameras, each camera view is scanned by the 12 inch monitor, but each individual camera has its own recording unit. One camera each for the two VCR-DVR units and two cameras each for the two GO.VIDEO dual deck VCR's. I also have a computer that can tag along and capture up to 4 more cameras, but I have lost evidence when computers lose power, the VCR won't do that. In a very large place like an Opera House investigation I will use the additional cameras and computer, but for small venues I just take the unit as pictured to capture EVP and video evidence.

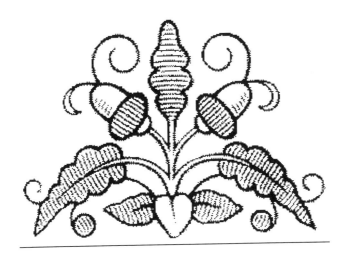

Chapter Five:

Simple, Yet Pointed Dialog

As I already stated, make an outline of what you want to say or do before you begin to record. In field investigations the dialog will be totally different than in a controlled studio or lab environment. Tailor your questions accordingly. Make sure if you're going to use an analog tape recorder that you use only new tapes and not previously recorded ones. I can fit 5 sessions on a single side of a 90 minute tape, and remember; cassette tapes can stretch and obscure what is really recorded on it so limit your tape purchase to 45 minutes or less per side. I found that the 120 minute (60 minutes per side) loose shape very quickly and distort what has been recorded. Some researchers record directly to their computer with audio software installed and USB microphones. Some of the best software to use is Voyetra Audio Surgeon, Audacity, EVP maker, Adobe Audition, Goldwave, Acoustica, and Cool Edit Pro. Most of these titles can be downloaded for a 30 day free trial, and some are a lot less expensive than others. My advice to you is, try them all, and purchase the one that you can understand and navigate well, no sense ending up with the most expensive software there is and not being able to understand how to use it properly.

I like to stay away from the multi-track software because I don't want anybody to say I faked it with a second track. And with all the other functions I found the software very tech heavy. I do own them, but I like to use Voyetra Audio Surgeon because of its ease of use. If you can navigate through Microsoft Word, you can use this software with ease. I started out with this product and often default to it again and again. Downloading cassette tapes or recording directly on to the program is a snap, and I paid less than 40 bucks for it. Now, keep in mind I record to cassette tape, and then transfer it to the computer if I find anything worth keeping via a 1/8 inch male at both ends cable for my hand held digital recorders and stereo RCA jacks to 1/8 inch male cable between my dual deck recorders and computer.

IN HOME EVP RESEARCH LAB DIALOG

Once you have decided which route you want to take, you still need to map out what course of action you will be taking during your sessions. You can write out anything you want to say, any questions you want answered. The following is what I use on a day to day basis now for my at home general dialog recordings and routine:

I always set my recording tape counter to 000 no matter where on the tape I happen to be, then begin recording, I also log the start time and end time as well as tag it audibly on the tape every session.

Turn on the recorder and wait at least 15 seconds before talking.

It is (day, date, time inserted here) and I am using cassette tape number (insert number and the A or B side). My name is John Douglas Gruber. "Today, as I seek communication with spirits who have passed from their lives on Earth, some of you may be drawn to my presence to ask for help or guidance. I want very much to help you, but must point out that I am but a mortal earth bound soul, and you are in spirit preparing for your further soul development. Spiritual law requires that you begin from within your own heart in the honest search for higher spiritual advancement and enlightenment. I assure you that seeking and asking for divine assistance will bring you peace and love of the highest order. You must be ready and willing for this to happen. There are many guiding spirits and divine entities who await your call. I am here to reassure you that there is a better place for you in the light. If you have a message to send that would help take a burden from you and help you cross over, tell me, let me know you are here, give me a simple sign that you have come to talk with me. You could simply speak into this box (point at mic here), and I can hear what you have to say. Talk to me, (pause for at least 5 seconds here) tell me what you want or need. "May I ask you some questions? (Pause here for at least 5 seconds) You do not have to answer any question that makes you feel uncomfortable. (You start your questions here, my example follows).

1. Is there anyone in this room with me right now?

2. Are you willing to speak with me today?

3. If you can't speak to me, could you move something or make a noise?

4. I have dominos here for you to knock over and communicate with me, could you knock over the domino number 2?

5. If you knock on something, let's use once for yes and twice for no.

6. Can you hear me very well?

7. Are you male?

8. Are you female?

9. Are there more people here than just you and I?

10. What is your name?

11. What year is it?

12. How old are you?

13. Did you live in Columbus, Ohio?

14. Did you work around here?

15. Were you in the Military?

16. Do you know anyone around here?

17. Do you have any family members with you?

18. Are there other family members I can talk with?

19. Have you talked with any of your relatives or friends?

20. Is there a message you want me to deliver to anyone?

21. Are you happy where you are right now?

22. Have you crossed over to the other side already?

23. Is it beautiful where you are?

24. Are there many others where you are?

25. Is anyone else here willing to talk with us today?

26. Have you ever talked with anyone in this manner before?

27. Does it make you feel tired to talk with me?

28. May I take pictures of you the next time we meet?

29. May I talk with you again, sometime?

30. Thank you for your time, and good day to you.

(Say this here). End this E.V.P. session at (insert end time, and tape counter end numbers here).

I always have an alternative method of communication setting in front of me just in case they cannot speak but can move things around. I have placed dominos on my desk starting with the number one on the left and ending with number six on the right in a straight row each standing on end. I have had them knocked over before along with the correct number I asked for. You could use a flashlight, a feather or empty Styrofoam cup, or anything else you choose. All my sessions are video taped now as well, because I have had things move and knocked over and I was caught way off guard. I also have a K2 and EMF meter on the desk turned on, and a digital thermometer permanently mounted on the wall above my desk. I do not state the opening dialog when I do field work, only in the lab in a controlled environment.

Again, this is just the outline of my game plan that I am using to give you an example; you use your own words and ideas for an opening statement and question dialog, whatever makes you the most comfortable.

When I first started to record home experiments, and this worked also, I did not use the meditation or call to the spirits dialog you just read, I used the following:

It is (day, date, time inserted here). My name is John Douglas Gruber. I am here today to talk to anyone who will speak to me from the other side. I am not here to hurt you in any way; in fact, I have nothing here that could harm you. All of the gadgets you see me use here are to help me listen and understand you. You can speak freely, without any worry of harm or traps. I will not attempt to make you cross over to the other side. You could simply speak into this box (point at mic here), and I can hear what you have to say. Please, if there is anyone listening to the sound of my voice, respond to me. Give me a sign that you can hear me. .May I ask you some questions? You do not have to answer any question that makes you feel uncomfortable.

1. Is there anyone in this room with me right now?

2. Are you willing to speak with me today?

3. If you can't speak to me, could you move something or make a noise?

4. If you knock on something, let's use once for yes and twice for no.

5. Can you hear me very well?

6. Are you male?

7. Are you female?

8. Are there more people here than just you and I?

9. What is your name?

10. What year is it?

11. How old are you?

12. Did you live in Columbus, Ohio?

13. Did you work around here?

14. Have you ever lived in this house?

15. Were you in the Military?

16. Do you know anyone around here?

17. Do you have any family with you?

18. Is there a message you want me to deliver to someone?

19. Are you happy where you are right now?

20. Are there other family members I can talk with?

21. Have you talked with your relatives or friends?

22. Have you crossed over to the other side already?

23. Is it beautiful where you are?

24. Are there many others where you are?

25. Is anyone else willing to talk with us today?

26. Have you ever talked with anyone in this manner before?

27. Does it make you tired to talk with me?

28. May I talk with you again, sometime?

29. May I take pictures of you the next time we meet?

30. Thank you for your time, and good day to you.

(Say this here). End this E.V.P. session at (insert end time, and tape counter end numbers here).

Scheduling:

I found that entities will speak on tape at any time of day or night no matter what phase the moon is in or if sun spots are present or not. In the beginning, however, it is advisable to record at a regular time and place, thus creating a routine. In doing this, the entities will quickly learn your recording time table. After making a connection with some entities, you will be able to capture EVP at any time and in any location. It took me around 30 to 45 days to collect my first EVP from home. Try to find a place that will be quiet, free of interruptions and a lot of natural background noise. Background sounds are okay if you use them, but it is up to you as to what volume level will work for you, it is important that you are aware of this so that you will recognize what sounds are natural and what sounds are EVP's. Always try to limit your natural background noise when you can. Keep your recordings short. You will want to listen to each part of the recording very carefully and this can take a lot time. My home sessions last about 8 to 9 minutes each.

Speak clearly, and methodically but not like a robot. Have compassion and sincerity in your dialog.

Recording:

Vocalize with sincerity all of your questions during an EVP session. Many investigators begin with a short prayer and an invitation to friends from the other side to participate in the experiment as I do. It can be helpful to begin an experiment by speaking your name and the date for the spirits sake as well as for a recorded permanent diary of sorts for your records. I have found that the entities will often come through as soon as the recorder is turned on. These beginning messages are often the loudest and clearest, so it is a good idea to turn on the recorder and wait a few seconds before announcing yourself and then ask your questions. Your questions should be recorded, and you should leave a period of time between each comment for the entities to respond. I discovered that it's best to leave at least 15-20 seconds of space in-between questions to give the Spirits time to form an answer. This goes for home lab or in the field experiments. All but the most seasoned investigators get impatient and don't give enough quiet time between questions. This will most assuredly skunk you every time, or you will be asking the next question right over the spirits direct response to your previous one.

Computer Recording:

You can use a computer for home recording, and a laptop or another type of computer that can be on the go for field work. Your computer should have an audio input jack, speakers, headphone jack and sound player application of some form. Windows comes with a Sound Recorder application that will work for recording but not for editing. A sound editing software like 'Voyetra Audio Surgeon', 'Adobe Audition' or 'Source Forge Audacity' are the most popular because these applications allow for easy amplification, filtering and reversing of the sound files. Source Forge Audacity is a free program that you can download from the internet.

You can make the recording on a tape recorder and then play the tape into a computer file for review, editing and storage as I do, or attach a microphone directly to the computer's microphone input jack or USB if your microphone is so equipped an then use the sound editor as your tape recorder.

When transferring into a computer, make sure the computer is set for "Line In" recording in "Sound and Multimedia" from the "Control Panel" of your Personal Computer, then connect the recording device with a 1/8 inch male stereo plug at each end to the "line in" jack of your computer. If you must transfer sound from the "Earphone" jack of your recorder instead of a regular output (which is the case with small hand held digital recorders), consider purchasing an "attenuating cord" to match the difference in resistance between the two jacks. I found that Radio Shack can help you with this configuration.

Digital Voice Recorders:

If you are using a digital voice recorder, I recommend that you listen to the playback on your computer. You will be surprised at the quality of the sound track when it is not listened to with the little built-in speakers that come with your recorder. You don't need to use an external microphone, as the recorders do not make any internal motor noise.

Should you decide to purchase a digital voice recorder for EVP, keep in mind that some investigators believe that cheap is good. Their theory is that the less expensive recorders usually use a lower sample rate, which produces more noise and it is that noise they believe, the entities use to form voices. The jury is still out for me on this one.

Playback:

The spirit or paranormal voice is usually not heard until playback of the tape or digital recorder, if you can hear it while you are recording, it is then called a VP (voice phenomenon). Investigators report that the voices tend to become stronger and clearer as the spirits gain in experience, but at first the voices may speak in whispers or at least very low levels. And as with my experience, the voices may not be recorded in every session and it may take several sessions for you to discover your very first voice. Hearing the voices is a learned ability and you will get better each and every time you listen. The entities seem to somehow learn through practice how to come through more frequently with strength and begin to increase in volume, and there answers seem to become more long winded, and precise.

Analyzing the Recordings for EVP:

Always use headphones when listening to the recordings on a computer.

The earmuff style that completely covers the ear (over the ear style) is best, but also good are the soft rubber ear buds that are inserted in the channel of the ear, I just won't be borrowing them from you.

Be sure to set up a method of saving your recordings in your computer that will allow you to easily locate your captured evidence for analysis. A good practice is to save the raw recording session in a dated folder, copy the raw file and save to the same folder. This is the sound file you will use to play with and listen to, leave the raw file alone and untouched. Then also save clips containing the EVP in the same folder making sure you label each file properly. Field recordings should be saved under the name and the date of the location where the evidence was collected, but still keeping a raw file that will go untouched. Using first and last names help to sort evidence in a folder for easy retrieval. The underline and dash symbol with no use of capitals helps assure that computer systems and the internet accept the file name. A 200 kb audio file can be reduced to around 15 Kb when converted from a *.wav file to an *.mp3 file. This makes it easy for sharing files via the Internet. You can find plenty of sites willing to authenticate you're collected evidence, and remember, always send the raw recorded evidence in a .wav file, not an mp3 file. I find that the mp3 files degrade the clarity. Make sure you send the raw file, just as it had been recorded, not your already enhanced cut & pasted version. It is ok to clip the segment, but leave about 30 seconds before and after the suspected evidence.

Keeping a Journal:

Maintaining records in a journal of recording sessions and results is a very helpful and useful tool and a must if you are going to get them authenticated. Include the date, time, tape number and tape side, weather information, and place on the counter where the message is received, the message itself, and the questions that were asked. Be sure to label the cassette tapes and its case if you do not use a digital recorder for easier archiving.

<u>Extra notes:</u>

Some home lab investigators make an 'appointment' with the intended Spirit the day before during prayer or meditation. Some also provide feedback before the session so that the spirits will know how the last experiment went and that their voices were indeed heard. It is not necessary to record in the dark. You will find that home lab investigators try different types of devices and energy sources to help the spirits communicate.

You may also want to put written questions in the EVP experiment area the day before. I am told the entities may read these and could respond accordingly. Also, they can hear your inner thoughts. You might want to say what you want to accomplish mentally several times over in your mind, but it's always best to ask your questions out loud during the actual recording period at home and in field research.

I have found that EVP may occur in any technology that will record sound and voices. With this in mind, it should be clear to you that there aren't really any rules when it comes to EVP evidence capture or collection. Mix it up for your initial trials and experiments, and find what works for you and what nets you the best results then stick to it, who cares which methods others use, this is your project and nothing to my knowledge has been set in stone in the field anyway. Who knows, you may be the breakthrough method we all end up using.

I also want to mention here that it is not uncommon for an EVP to contain a voice recognizable by you of a discarnate person thought to be speaking to you in an EVP. It is also common for that entity to say something that would be typical of what he or she's personality traits would have said while they were in the physical world. Their personality clearly remains intact even though the person no longer occupies a physical body, or walks this earthly plane. This is a wonderful event so don't get freaked out if you know them.

FIELD STUDY AND INVESTIGATION DIALOG

In remote locations or investigative sites and in homes, you would use a completely different approach to your EVP sessions. Some people know this as a "call and response" session, others just go by EVP session. Remember, just because you don't feel, see or hear anything in an area or room does not mean you shouldn't record an EVP session. I have captured many disembodied voices to my surprise in a spot I felt there wouldn't even be a fly buzz.

Standards of Practice:

1. During an EVP session, only one person should ask the questions at a time.

2. Whispering is not allowed during an EVP session or during an investigation. In fact, I will ask you to leave the session. Period!

3. Any ambient sounds, coming from an investigator or the environment, should be indentified or "tagged" on the audio recording immediately after they are heard or created.

4. If an investigator experiences something interesting or unexplained during the EVP session, they should speak to point out this occurrence. Other than that, all investigators should remain completely quiet, except for the specified questioner.

5. During the evidence review, potential EVP should be verified by at least one other digital recording source. This is to help eliminate natural sources for the sounds. This source can be another audio recorder in the room or from a video source recording the event. This step is vital when attempting to verify the authenticity and credibility of the data.

6. The following are examples of questions to ask during a field EVP session. Questions with strictly a yes or no answer should be kept to a minimum. And you should keep the questions to no less than 10 and no more than 15.

Is there anyone here that would like to talk to us?

May I record what you have to say?

Can you tell us your name?

How old are you?

Why are you here?

Are you sad or angry?

Are you alone?

How many of you are here?

What is your favorite color?

Do you know what year it is?

Can you tell us what happened to you?

Can you see us?

What do we look like?

What color is your hair?

Do you know my name?

Would you like us to leave?

Is there any way that we can help you?

Can you show us what you look like?

Is someone keeping you here?

Are you afraid where you are?

Do you have anything to tell us?

Can you do anything to let us know you are here?

What time of day is it right now?

Are you married?

What is your spouse's name?

What year were you born?

Do you have children?

What are their names?

How old are they?

What is your occupation?

Do you enjoy it?

Is it beautiful where you are?

How are you feeling?

Is there anything in particular that you would like to do?

Do you know who we are?

How do you feel about us being here?

Is there anything we can do for you?

Can I take your picture?

Would you make a sound or knock to show us where you are?

Do you know today's date?

Who is the president of the United States right now?

Can we talk with you again some other time?

Is this your home?

How long have you been here?

Are you here all the time?

What is your favorite room in this house?

Is there anyone else here?

What are their names?

Where were you born?

Did you grow up in this area?

Where did you live?

Do you have family here?

Are you afraid of us?

Will you let us help you?

Would you like a priest to be here?

Pick and choose from the list above or come up with your own questions. You may want to even tailor your questions according to the investigative site.

I want to say here that I do not believe in provoking, in my personal opinion it makes for great TV, but I am not going to bark orders to my grandmother, father, mother, or anybody else's loved one that has died I happen to come in contact with. I wouldn't respond to your shouting if I was a spirit, but it's up to you. I do not allow the act of provoking from within my team without an argument. My question is how can you help a spirit with his or her dilemma if you have made them angry? What kind of time are you going to have if you end up trying to cross this spirit over? Plus, every time I have been screamed at, ordered around and then told to leave, I say "make me", I am a human, I think I pretty much have the same reaction that most of you would. Just think about it before you go off provoking, what can of worms are you potentially going to open for a psychic on your team when he or she tries to help the lost spirit or soul find peace in the light? We all don't want an investigation to go violent, so why should we be the ones to instigate it first? Ok. I am down off my soap box now. This is your gig, your experiments and investigations; you make yourself happy, I just wanted to let you know how I feel and what I think about provoking. And I am compelled to say that if you run into a spirit that needs or wants to cross over into the light, you should be obligated to do so. It is not healthy or right to just gather evidence from them and not help in this task. You must be immensely dedicated and completely grounded to provide this service. There are many groups out there that rescue spirits all the time, just get in contact with one in your area and ask for their help, if you or no one in your group has accomplished this before or knows how.

Be careful not to fall into the trappings of EVP's by just continually connecting to the same spirit for your results, and not caring what happens to them. If they ask for your help, during the one or two initial sessions, assure them that you will be getting them help and then do it. The field is crawling with experts that will be more than willing to help you and the spirit. I have had some luck with local clergy, but finding that "in tune" open minded priest or reverend is a chore, although it can be done. Getting in contact with clergy and letting them know what you are doing before you do it is advisable. Talk to local priests and ask them if you ever need them to help a lost soul cross over to the light, would they help? I would be willing to bet they would be more than glad to help you, if they deem you serious. It always comes down to passion for the field, and how professional you are doesn't it? Most psychic mediums worth their weight will help you in this endeavor at no charge too, but if they want to charge you, find a different one. Their gift is from God, they should be very willing to help one of God's children find his or her way to the Holy White Light and enter, and the psychic shouldn't make you pay a toll for this task. This is why they got the gift in the first place isn't it, to help? Not to charge $500 bucks to profit from lost souls or spirits. I have never run in to one that has asked or states up front that they get paid for their services. Most legitimate psychics will not have a sign posted on their web site, or a business card that reads,

Investigating Haunted houses…$200.
Crossing a Spirit Over………..…$500.
Banishing a Demon………….$1000.
(Cash only please)

Chapter Six: 6

Fire it up!

Your ready, you have bought your new equipment for the home EVP lab, or for paranormal EVP field work and now it is time for you to fire it up. You got your opening statement prepared, your questions are in order and rehearsed, you're anxious and nervous, but still all ready to go. Here are some tips that have helped me successfully capture EVP's in both the home and in the field.

The first and most important information I can give you is treat every EVP session with the complete confidence that you are recording actual spirit communication. If you become complacent with your dialog or total session, you will quickly lose interest in your intentions and so will the spirits. You will not get evidence every time you record; in fact when it comes to the home lab, it can take over 30 daily sessions to get the first one. The spirits have to become comfortable with you, know that you care, and trust you. And make sure you have an alternate form of communication in front of you and ready to be moved around, I got the dominos to move way before the vocal communication was collected in my research. Never talk bad about the spirits earthly life, always have respect for them, after all, their dead. Whatever they did in their earthly life is gone, they just want peace now, and just might be asking you to help them achieve it.

Don't be surprised if the first few in home lab EVP's you collect are friends and family of yours as this is very common. As I stated before, the sound of their voice, or mannerisms can be very prevalent during the recording, and yet they could be giving you answers to your questions and not sound a thing like your loved one. I always test the spirits that say they know me by asking some questions that only the friend or loved one the spirit claims to be and I would know the answer to.

Remember, no matter what method you're using, home lab, field investigations, background noise, no noise, analog or digital recorders, TV image loops and whatever else you my try, do yourself a huge favor and may be your team mates too, test the equipment over and over again until you are completely confident that you know how it operates, and that you can do this flawlessly. Record you children, your dog, the television or radio, then download it to the computer, analyze it, save it in a raw file that won't be touched and play around with a copy. Practice what you're going to say until it rolls off your tongue. If you do happen to get mundane about it, mix up the dialog, ask new questions, rewrite your introduction or even change the routine recording session time of the day. I found that I got sounding like a robot and changed a few things around, then was taken completely by surprise when I got one of the best EVP's I have ever recorded. You never know when it is going to happen, so never let your guard down, be prepared for the unexpected 100% of the time.

Make sure you allow the recorder to run at least 15 seconds before you start your dialog, many strong EVP's have been captured in this quiet time segment. Be sincere in asking your questions and be sure that you wait at least a full 15 to 20 seconds between each one. Tag everything you do that makes a noise on the recorder, from "I dropped my pen" to "I burped", this only makes it a heck of a lot easier to analyze the recording later. Be aware of all the natural background noise like airplanes, mailmen and such, and tag them all as they happen. After you have listened to hours upon hours of recordings looking for evidence, you will come to appreciate the investigator that tags every little sound or bump in the night that he or she has heard or created. If you become a great tagger, your playback listening will be a breeze compared to someone who doesn't.

I realize that all of the kinks should have been worked out when you went through the dry runs with your equipment, but it couldn't hurt to recheck all of your connections and settings one more time before you start your sessions for real.

For the in home lab, make sure all of the cables are connected. The mixing board has your microphone plugged in to the first channel, or channel one and that the other end of the cable is completely connected to the microphone. If your particular model of microphone has an on/off switch, make sure it is in the on position. Double check to see that the phantom power switch on the sound mixer is also in the on position, and that the channel volume controls as well as the master volume are set at the proper levels you used for your tests. Leave the "high" and "low" control knob on flat (this is the 12 o'clock position), but turn the "trim" knob up full. Keep the "mon" or monitor and the "FX" knob (if you're mixing board has this one), at the off position. Always keep the master "FX to Main" control on the main mixer panel to the off position. If your unit comes with an "EQ" or built in stereo graphic equalizer, always bypass this feature or set it to flat 0.

Check to see that the record out cords are connected to the mixing board in the correct jacks (red to red and black to black), and that the other end is connected in the same manner on your dual cassette tape deck's line in jacks. Ok and this one may sound silly but, make sure every power cord is plugged into a working outlet. You should have selected the record level on your tape deck during your trials, so make sure it is in the exact position you want before your session starts, as turning up this level during recording effects the quality of the sound. Again, only use a fresh 90 minute cassette tape and be sure to label it and enter it in to your journal. Always plug in your headphones to the recorder only; you want to hear the way the recording will sound with the levels on the tape deck, not the mixer. What you hear from the mixer is not what is being recorded. Keep a watchful eye on the volume

VU meters or led lights to make sure you don't go into the red areas during your dialog. By the led or VU needle going in to the red, your voice will sound distorted and over modulated and this should be avoided since you want the clearest recording you can get. Make sure you stay at least two or three feet away from the microphone when you record. Don't worry, these microphones can pick up in a 25 to 30 foot 360° radius quite well, enough to hear a pin drop at 20 feet, I tested it. And I know I have said this way too often, but always wait at least 15 seconds after you turn on the recorder before you start any dialog, or time and date stamping.

I had a few things go wild while I was recording, in the visual sense not audio that caught me so off guard and I felt like a complete idiot when it was over. I have an old 3 inch rusted sleigh bell hanging from a ribbon in my lab, and it has become quite the "spirit give me a sign" item. It swings easily, makes noise and is about 6 inches to the right of my computer screen so I could hardly miss it. During one session, the bell started swing and hitting the wall, shaking and sounding off. I had never anticipated anything like this, never. I scrambled to get a camcorder, and it became very clear instantly that I didn't have film in it and there and no external battery was attached. Arrggghh! I became completely frustrated, and grabbed the digital still camera and started snapping away, then duh; it has a video setting to take up to 5 minutes worth of video complete with sound. I was all over it, yea right. I call this my "three stooges" routine EVP session. My God, it was a mess. Well, I got my audio recording without any voices, (except a few choice words to vent my anger at my unpreparedness), but I did get some great snapshots and the 5 minutes of video and sound. I think what really bites is I had this really great visual paranormal event happening right before my eyes, and I was loaded for bear for just audio recording, I never imagined I would get something like this. How un-thoughtful I was, I was in the mindset that I was after audio EVP's never giving it a second thought that something visual might just happen to occur. So now I have one of my night vision surveillance cameras I use in the field investigations, mounted near the ceiling in the far corner of my lab, attached to a VCR to record each and every EVP session I have. I will not be taken by surprise ever again. We learn to modify the methods by trial and error, and I gained a great insight from my huge mistake that day.

Now you don't have to go to this extreme, but I will tell you to at least have a camera or camcorder handy and ready to go just in case something visually spectacular happens during your session. Keep in mind that you should use the adapter for a wall plug while utilizing your camcorder as the spirits like to drain batteries, so you could be scrambling to insert new batteries in your device instead of taking in the cool stuff.

Now, let's get on to the field investigation aspect of EVP recording. It is always advisable to set the hand held digital recorder next to you on a table, chair window ledge or even on the floor. This keeps the "moving around in your hands" noise that you will get recorded to a bare minimum. Set the volume control to a desired level, (test this in the room or area you are in as it changes from venue to venue.) Again, leave at least the first 15 seconds blank and then begin by stating the date and time, your name and any other investigators who are with you and where you are conducting the session and a case number if you or your group requires one. Once you start asking your questions, try to stay still, many of the footsteps recorded can end up being your own or another investigator in the room. Be sure to leave at least 15 seconds between the questions to allow the spirit or spirits time to form words for a message. The digital recorder has different files or folders you can place your recordings in, and most automatically place the sessions in a distinct single numbered file or folder. This makes your journal entries much easier to maintain and refer back to. Refrain from using the pause feature between sessions. Always conclude your session by stating "end this EVP session" and then press the stop button. This will always be a help in your research to keep the rooms or areas captured or collected EVP's completely separated. If you are a member of an investigative group, your director may have set protocol and questions to be asked and you should not deviate from these rules and guidelines. Each group has a certain way they want things done, or what has worked for them in the past and you should follow their instructions explicitly.

If you are going it alone though, you should transfer your recordings to the computer after the investigation is over right away, and don't clear the digital recorder until you have saved all the new files in a folder on your computer and are sure they work. This keeps things from being inadvertently erased off the recorder or being recorded over. Each file on the digital recorder should have its own file on your computer and labeled. Ok, the best way to label and save a file on your computer is as a *.wav file and the label should have no capital letters in it and no spaces.

"EVP Session 1" is not a proper file name, it should be labeled in this manner "evp_session_1" and saved as a *.wav file to be able to download to the internet much smoother without having any complications or errors. After is has been saved the file should look like this "evp_session_1.wav" and always use the raw untouched version for the original. You should make a copy of the raw file to play with on your sound editing software, never use the original raw recording, put this file in a safe place and even copy it to a disk or folder that is marked "do not touch." I keep my *.wav files, notes and case study folders under "SPATS CASES" in specific sub folders on my computer under the label of the clients name. For example; in the Smith folder you will find the following sub folders; Client information, History Research, Picture evidence, Video evidence, EVP evidence, Miscellaneous and Results. The evidence files will be in there corresponding sub folder.

Chapter Seven: 7

Revising the Game Plan

There comes a time when sessions become stale and non-productive. If this happens, it is time to revise your strategy. Changes should be subtle, nothing major all at once. Try changing your dialog, or opening statement first, and give it a few days. If this does not yield any results, try changing the background noise if you are using it, or add the background noise if you aren't using it already. Again, let these changes have a few days 5 to 10 perhaps, to see if they will spark anything new. I really tried the background noise to no avail. After I got absolutely no result for over 60 daily EVP sessions, I abandoned the white noise background altogether. The most important thing with successful capture or collection of EVP recording is having the patience to cope with many days of getting no action at all. Sometimes you may get results right away and other times it will be like banging your head against the wall leaving you to wonder why you started these experiments at all.

Make sure you are not getting any EVP's by listening to the cassette tape or files on your computer again. On average it takes about two to three weeks of experiments and sessions before you get anything. But, make sure that you are not getting anything, and that you are not just missing what you have already gotten. It takes a long time to train your ear to distinguish a spirit communication voice. Some of the voices are as soft as a whisper, low and tonal in pitch, and could be either slower or faster than normal speech, with words pronounced and accentuated strangely.

Once you begin collecting real EVP's it is a great idea to try to continue with the same routine and method for at least one continuous month as the voices tend to continue once they start, or until the communications slow or quit. The equipment you are using and the method of dialog can produce voices lasting for many weeks or months, and then without warning just stop for a short period of time, a few weeks or even months. But, it will pick up again, and during the "desert period" when nothing is being received, it is a great time to update equipment, and look over or perhaps revise your dialog.

Actually there is nothing mysterious about recording EVP. It is just a matter of if the voices are present or not.

The basic techniques are simple, straightforward, and the equipment is easy to handle and readily available. There is one experimenter named Dave that uses one of those little desktop therapy waterfall features on his recording desk during his sessions. The sound of the water trickling is a sort of pink noise, (like they use in the Malls to keep people noise down) and he maintains great results which he attributes to the water feature. I have gotten a lot of email about the use of the mini portable cassette recorders for EVP lab and field work. Folks, these recorders are not recommended due to the high motor noise captured by the built in microphone. Now you can add on a microphone, but get a good one with at least 10 to 20 feet of cable. And be sure it is an omni-directional dynamic or digital one, not a condenser microphone as they have a tendency to cause echoes and random hissing sounds. Make sure you use every bit of that cable between the microphone and the mini cassette deck to minimize the noise being captured on the recorder. And again, if you want even a fighting chance of collecting any evidence you must use a fresh brand new 90 minute cassette tape.

Revisit the preparatory process that you have been using for your EVP sessions. Always keep in mind that the nonphysical entities are present and able to witness all of your activity, they don't just show up when it is recording time. Routine, routine, routine! It is the best method to consistently collect EVP's. You could play the same music or song to indicate to the spirits that you are about to begin your session. When the song ends, announce you're starting now and turn on the recorder, wait the 15 seconds and then begin your dialog. I had a gentleman send me an email that nothing he had tried to do has worked, so I asked him to send me a recording of his complete recording session. I mean from the time he walked into the lab till the time he left the room. Well, he did this for me, and boy was I surprised at what I heard. First, I opened the file and I could hear him opening the door and walking in the room. He tagged the recording for me stating that he was now seated in his office chair at the recording table. He then proceeded to describe what he was doing and turned on some music. During the music playing, he stated loud and clear, "now this song you dumb asses should like!" I turned off the tape and never listened to another word. Are you kidding me, is that what you consider kind, compassionate, and caring dialog? I don't believe he will ever get voices on his recorder, do you?

Make sure you're not making the same mistake in your dialog or even in your lab before you're dialog or tape recorder even starts. One cannot expect results when you insult the very spirit you are trying to reach. This is why I light candles, say a prayer and meditate before I start my sessions. I guess you could call it seducing the spirit, or at least calming them, reassuring them that I am serious. Take a long hard look at your actions before, during and after your routine. Make a few little subtle changes if you want to, or make one large change in the way you warm up, begin, middle, or end your sessions. Remember, a little change is good but completely gutting the whole thing and started over could set you back considerably. Gaining the trust of spirits is the name of the EVP game. You may want to even ask questions to the spirits about how to improve your dialog to get better recordings. Who knows, they might just give you a really cool answer.

You could zero in on an event in their life, or you might even use the shanghai method, (the use of their era music, period dress, or historic radio show sound waves, or even an old television show playing in the background that was present during the time they were walking upon this earthly plane) to spark dialog or conversation. They have been known from time to time to give comment on the props you are using to coax them into an interaction. It is easy to find radio show sound clips and bites, or you can purchase or record an old movie and have it playing from a DVD or VCR to a small television set in you lab.

Again, these are just some suggestions to initiate dialog between you and the spirits, use any or all of these puzzle pieces to help in your research. Use whatever could work for you, just mix it up and have fun. But, if whatever you are presently doing is gaining results, don't mess with it. I just want you to know that there are different avenues to take if you are idle and the spirit voice recordings have stopped. It can really be fun for you and the spirit if you use some of these methods, to keep things fresh and exciting. I had correspondence with a female experimenter that had her kids catch about 12 butterflies and let them fly around the lab, because the spirit she had encountered loved to catch and catalog them when she was younger. It worked! The spirit came through immediately and began classifying the species of the flying creatures during the EVP session, and commenting on how beautiful they all were. Not only did her kids have fun, but they also became involved in the EVP experiment with their mother. She played the recording back for her children and the kids were very excited. A win, win in my way of thinking. And I am sure that the spirit (named Anna) had a ball too. Sure beats the heck out of "talk to me now, I demand that you show me a sign!" and "show me that you're here, I don't believe in you, I dare you too!" By the way, the butterflies were recaptured and released back into their environment I am assured, just in case you were wondering.

Chapter Eight: 8

Analyzing the Results

Are you ready to analyze your recordings? Before beginning you will need a few basic items.

First you will need a personal computer or laptop that has multimedia programs and capabilities with an updated operating system. Then you will need to install some sound editing software. There are a lot of choices for this software which comes with a huge range in price. Many are free to try for 30 days, but are restricted in what you can do during the trial period. Make sure that whatever title of software you purchase or download is completely compatible with your computer and its operating system. I have found that many of these programs are not compatible with a Mac, although some of the higher end ones are.

Audio Analysis & Record keeping

Any audio recorder no matter if it is analog or digital that has a headphone socket can be connected to a desktop or laptop computer that is equipped with a built in or added sound card as long as it has the proper input and output jacks. Connect the appropriate size audio lead from your digital recorder's headphone socket directly to the line in socket on your computer and you are ready to go with your field recorded evidence. Many of the newer digital recorders on the market have the ability to load files to a computer via a USB port. Always capture your recordings with a software program and label the very first file as "raw" which tells you not to touch this one with any of the filters or tools from within the analyzing program. I copy the "raw" file and always play with this one, never the original sound recording and I don't erase the hand held recorder until later.

Never erase the pure recording from your recorder until the down loaded files, both the "raw" and copy are good. I have a file system for all my recordings, findings and such and keep them in a separate folder in this manner for field work. Click on documents, then right click and open a new folder. Name this folder as you wish, mine is SPATS. Then open this folder and create two new folders and name them as you see fit, mine are client and research. Under the folder named "client" add another two new folders with mock client names, mine are "The Smiths" and "The Clines" as shown below. Under each of these you can add as many sub-folders as you want and name them however you like, mine is "Recorded Evidence", "Picture Evidence" and so on.

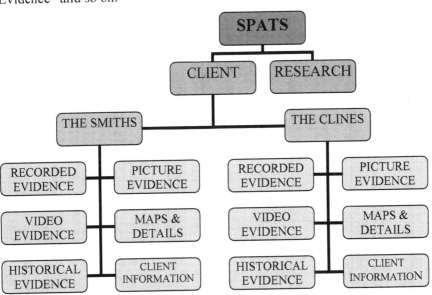

I add people to the client folder by their names and then put the evidence in the corresponding folder. The "raw" EVP session recording goes in the recorded evidence folder along with its copy that I can analyze, the pictures go in the picture evidence folder well, you get the idea. You can set up your folders and sub-folders any way you like as long as you can keep them straight and make it as un-confusing as you can for you.

Now when it comes to the lab research evidence, I use a different approach.

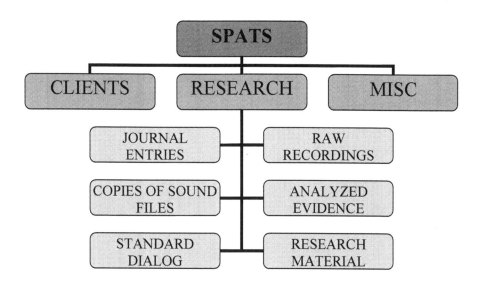

I keep all of the original recordings time and date stamped of course, in the folder marked "RAW RECORDINGS", that way I am not tempted to goof around with them using the software. If I over analyze or ruin a collected EVP, I simply discard it and make a copy of the "raw" one and start over. I am not trying to get you to follow my procedures exactly, just trying to give you examples of how to do your record keeping in a methodical way. Choose any number of files and name them anyway you would like.

Your recordings can be analyzed sufficiently in software programs that can be purchased on line or over the counter at your favorite computer software store. Once your recorder is connected from the headphone or mixer line out to the line in jack on your computer, press the record button in your chosen software program and press play on your audio recorder simultaneously; your sound file will now be loading to the analysis program. Whatever the volume level of the recorder is set to will determine the decibel level of the sound file that is loaded on to the computer. If you find that your recordings are not loud enough after loading them on to your computer, simply turn up the volume level on the recorder and reload the audio file. It is easier to listen to the recordings if each session is kept in a separate file.

Now that your recordings have been loaded to computer, you are able to listen to them, break them down and save them accordingly. You can also use features in the software programs such as hiss reduction, noise reduction, amplify and various filters that can be used to enhance the quality of any inexplicable voices contained your files. These features should be used sparingly and the recordings should be kept as close to their raw state as possible. And keep in mind; never use the "raw" or original file for enhancing. Using these features too much on any recording is deemed 'over processing' and can damage your file copy. You will know that you have 'over processed' a recording when it becomes difficult on the ear, which is when the 'Undo' feature comes in very handy! Equally, these features can be extremely useful if used correctly, so please take time to experiment with and learn as much as you can about the software you are using. Much information can also be learned about your recordings within the software itself with features such as frequency analysis and spectral views.

I recommend the use of headphones or a set of ear buds during analysis, although, please be aware of any sudden loud noises that occur during your recordings which could cause damage to your ears. Keep the volume to a comfortable level until you believe you have caught something, and then you could increase the volume level and replay what you think you have. You will find that over a period of time you will develop an ear for hearing the distinct fast rhythm of an EVP voice and you will naturally start to focus on other levels of noise within your recordings that you may have never noticed previously. I compare this to listening to someone that speaks with a foreign accent, you may find them difficult to understand at first, but the more you listen to them the more you get used to the distinct nature of their voice and comprehend what they are saying. If you find that you have not successfully recorded any inexplicable voices then please persevere, you will find that during experimentation you will gradually receive more and more voices.

Once you capture that first elusive voice, there is no holding back. For best results, I always recommend recording regularly at the same time of day, I know I have said this already but it is true. It is very much like opening a doorway and waiting for somebody to walk through. After their first visit, they may return many times if the doorway is welcoming and opened regularly, heck, they may even tell their friends! You can keep individual short clips of EVP's in another file but make sure you label them correctly.

As I stated a few pages ago, many different software programs are available for download and purchase that can be used to process your EVP recordings. **Here is some currently available Analyzing & Noise Software for EVP's** All of the information here is from the software product websites including the prices as of January 1, 2010.

EVP Assistant Software

EVP Assistant was designed by Mark Andrew Turner of the EVP Research Association UK as a basic noise generator for use with Electronic Voice Phenomena experiments. The featured noises can be played through your desktop PC or laptop speakers as a carrier sound for inter frequency experiments. The featured noises are white noise, pink noise, brown noise, waterfall and Spiricom. EVP Assistant is a flash based program that allows you to play the featured noises alone or together in any combination for 30 minutes at a time. The Spiricom noise was taken from original recordings by George Meek and William O'Neil. Due to the frequency of this noise, we do not recommend listening to it for long periods of time. The Spiricom noise fades out then back in again every 30 seconds, this goes on continually for 30 minutes and was designed this way because the noise can be quite exhausting to listen to. Combining the Spiricom noise with other noises featured in EVP Assistant can make for some interesting experiments. Free

EVP Gold Software

Our goal was to develop a fully-featured software program that would be easy for anyone--even computer newbie's--to operate. But we also wanted a program that would have all of the other options, bells, and whistles the more expensive packages had. You can import EVPs, export EVPs, and 'clean up' EVPs by taking out the background noise. This PC-based program does it all! This software sells at $97 (compare to $397 Adobe Audition--the software that TAPS uses--and you'll see what a true bargain this really is)!

Audio Surgeon Software

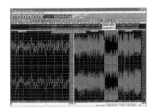

Take your digital music to the next level! Record it, edit it, transform it, convert it, manipulate it, and burn it to CD! Audio Surgeon lets you get inside your digital music files for the ultimate in customization and control. Optimize loudness, remove unwanted sections, fades in or out songs, removes hiss, use sound effects and more. You can even convert your music files to and from multiple file formats, such as MP3, WMA and WAV. It's the ultimate audio recording, editing and CD burning tool! 29.99

MixCraft by Acoustica Software

Record your own song or do some creative audio editing. This multi-purpose audio recording software is easy enough to jump into and powerful enough to make your own music hits! 64.95

WavePad Sound Editor Software

 Professional audio editing software for PC & Mac

This sound editing software is a full featured professional audio and music editor for Windows and Mac OS X. It will let you record and edit music, voice and other audio recordings. When editing audio files you can cut, copy and paste parts of recordings then add effects like echo, amplification and noise reduction. WavePad works as a wav or mp3 editor but it also supports a number of other file formats including vox, gsm, wma, real audio, au, aif, flac and ogg. We make this program free because we know you will love it so much you will want to upgrade to WavePad Master's Edition which has additional effects and features for the serious sound engineer. Download WavePad Master's Edition demo or purchase the WavePad Master's Edition version. From $39.95

Acoustica 4 Software

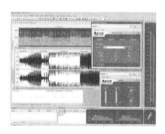 Acoustica 4 is an ideal solution for audio editing and mastering. The program contains everything you need to create great sounding recordings and audio CDs, including professional tools for recording, analysis, editing and CD burning. The Acoustica user interface was designed with speed, accuracy and ease of use in mind. The support for audio resolutions up to 32 bit and sampling rates up to 192 kHz allows you to record and edit in an amazing audio quality. A large range of high quality audio tools and effects are integrated in Acoustica including tools for dynamic processing, equalizing, numerous effects such as reverb, chorus and flange, as well time stretching and key transposition tools.

Recordings distorted by noise, clicks, crackle, clipping or missing high frequency content can be restored. The support for DirectX and VST plug-ins allows you to use tools and effects from other third party manufacturers directly from Acoustica.

AVS Audio Software

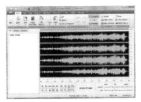

Editor Edit Audio

Cut, join, trim, mix, delete parts, split. Use Timeline for maximum precision and accuracy. Multichannel audio files are supported. Enhance Audio over 20 built-in effects and filters including delay, flange, chorus, reverb, and more. Full support of VST effects and DirectX filters. This software comes with Microsoft Windows 7 Support. All is Free

EVPmaker Software

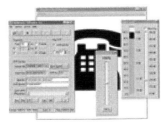

EVPmaker is experimental software for the generation of acoustic "raw material" for recordings of paranormal voices on tape, also known as "Electronic Voice Phenomena" (EVP). For this purpose, the program divides any recording of speech into short segments and then plays them back continuously in randomly order. The resulting "gibberish" still sounds like speech, but can't be understood anymore, and is therefore suited as background noise for EVP recordings. Of course, the program can also be used to generate special acoustical or musical effects. Free

GoldWave Software

 GoldWave is a highly rated, professional digital audio editor. It's fully loaded to do everything from the simplest recording and editing to the most sophisticated audio processing, restoration, enhancements, and conversions. It is easy to learn and use, so get started now by downloading the free, fully functional evaluation version! Price $19.95 for one year, $49.95 for lifetime.

Cool Edit Pro Software

(This is no longer produced but is still for sale everywhere on the internet)

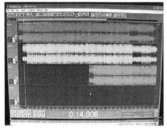 Cool Edit Pro is a multitrack digital audio recorder, editor, and mixer for Windows NT, 95, 98, and Windows XP. To use it, you need only a PC compatible computer running one of these operating systems, one or more Windows-compatible sound cards, and the desire to create some great audio.

Designed as a complete audio environment, Cool Edit Pro puts into one package all the functionality you need to take an audio project from concept to completion. You can use Punch In and record multiple takes to get each track just right, and Cool Edit Pro's support for multiple sound cards gives you complete freedom in routing your audio. Once you've recorded your tracks (up to 64 tracks!), you can apply Cool Edit Pro's unmatched DSP and editing power to tweak individual tracks and add the effects you need. When you're ready to mix, snap-to guides, crossfades, and separate level, pan, mute, and solo controls for each track will help you get it done.

While Cool Edit Pro provides an all-in-one audio solution, it also works with the rest of your audio tools as part of your studio. Support for Microsoft's DirectX/ActiveMovie protocol means you can use DSP modules from leading manufacturers like Waves and QTools from within Cool Edit Pro. If your needs go beyond digital audio to include working with MIDI or video, you will find Cool Edit Pro's MIDI/SMPTE synchronization provides seamless integration with these media. Though Cool Edit Pro is loaded with features, it doesn't encumber you with excess windows. You can get at just the features you want, and you don't need a 20-inch monitor and four hands to get the job done, because Cool Edit Pro's flexible but uncluttered interface offers a wide variety of controls (like right-click support for almost any object) that keep the main screen clean and efficient. You will find this under-the-hood architecture throughout Cool Edit Pro. Price ranges from free to over $299. In the U.S.A.

Cool Edit Pro is now Adobe Audition 2.0 Software

 Adobe Systems Incorporated acquired the technology assets of Syntrillium Software in May 2003 and introduced Adobe® Audition® software (a rebranded release of Cool Edit Pro) in August 2003. Adobe Audition 2.0 is the most current version of the software, and Syntrillium's other products have been discontinued. The same team has also released a public beta of Adobe Soundbooth, a brand new audio application built in the spirit of Sound Edit 16 and Cool Edit 2000. It uses a task-based interface that is specifically designed so that video editors, designers, and others without a background in audio can get their audio tasks done quickly. Download it now and leave your feedback on the Soundbooth public beta forums. Thanks to all who supported Syntrillium and Cool Edit Pro. We look forward to your support of Adobe Audition. $289.

Adobe Audition 3 Software

 Sound your best

Recording, mixing, editing, and mastering — Adobe® Audition® 3 software is the all-in-one toolset for professional audio production.

Use Adobe Audition 3 to:

•Create your own music

•Record and mix a project

•Produce a radio spot

•Clean up audio for a movie

•Compile and edit a soundtrack

Whatever you do with audio, Adobe Audition 3 software helps you sound your best. $349.00

Adobe® Soundbooth® CS4 software

 Create and edit audio with ease

Adobe® Soundbooth® CS4 software gives web designers, video editors, and other creative professionals the tools to create and polish audio, customize music, add sound effects, and do much more. Multitrack support and volume matching save you time Soundbooth CS4 now allows you to work on more than one mono or stereo file at a time. In addition, third-party research shows volume matching across multiple clips saves significant production time. $199.00

Additional white noise and market day crowd background noise is available from a lot of different sources. I found a really good crowd noise on the AAEVP web site free to download. You just have to loop it yourself.

Chapter Nine: 9

Success in a Nut Shell

Capturing EVP's is quite easy and in my thinking, very fun and exciting. You never know whose voice will come through on your recording, and the anticipation builds with each and every attempt and capture. I was becoming discouraged early on in my research, but quickly got motivated once more when the class "A" EVP's started showing up.

The best success with my in home lab research that I have accomplished has been when my confidence, determination and a daily routine started working like a well oiled machine. I got to the point where I couldn't wait till I got into the next session just to see what great thing might happen. I did add the video taping of all sessions just because I was taken completely off guard with the movement of the rusty bell in answer to several of my questions. I have since gotten the dominos to move or be knocked over numerous times during my question and answer sessions, and the specific numbers I asked for too! As I stated before, you do not have to go to this extreme if you don't want to, the choice is yours. I do suggest the placement of some kind of alternate method for communication beside the voice recorder. You may be able to capture a spirit talking on the recorder a few days or weeks after they have been giving you answers with your alternate method. It takes a while to build trust with the spirits, and soon you will be known as the go-to person in the spirit world to get their messages across.

To even have half a chance in being successful you need to get good solid equipment for your lab. Even if you choose to do field research, the equipment and the knowledge to use it is key. Be sure you use your head, stay calm and be courteous to the spirits and your other team mates.

Always be respectful of the dead, and not just in the recording session. If you are in a group that does investigations in the field, respect the routine they have mapped out for you and don't become a pain in the butt team member. Everyone's radar is in full swing on an investigation, and emotions run far and wide so they don't need to worry about what you are going to say or do at the site, keeping them from completing a successful evidence collection. Be professional and sincere if you are in someone's home trouncing though rooms gathering evidence of the paranormal in their otherwise private spaces. Be very respectful of the home owner's privacy and don't let the neighbors, media or internet share the unfortunate events exposing your client to ridicule and undue stress from the non-believing public. Don't wear offensive clothes or perfumes and always be polite. Keep the equipment in clean and good working order, store it properly and do not manhandle or be reckless with your or anybody else's equipment. The client will see this behavior and may feel they have made a big mistake in asking you into their home. And by all means do not freak out and go running out of the house screaming if you are touched, see, hear or are startled by something paranormal or not. These clients are putting all of their eggs in one basket with you and your team so if you appear worried or scared as a professional that does this all the time, think how they will feel.

Become that great team member that "tags" every detail during your recordings. The people who listen to the recorded sessions to find evidence will be very appreciative of that. Even for your home lab, tagging will quickly become your favorite thing after you listen over and over to your recordings for any anomalous sounds. Always ask your questions in either venue with sincerity and conviction. Have compassion for the spirit you wish to communicate with and speak clearly, don't yell and for heaven's sake, don't provoke! That's all you need, a spirit that has entered your home and you have made them angry and now they won't leave.

And if you are afraid of the dark, do not choose to be a field paranormal investigator. Stick to the home lab and conduct your sessions during the daylight hours. A moon is still full though out the day, tides rise and fall in the day time as you will notice if you are watching the lunar phases closely.

As new equipment is introduced to the public, try to upgrade if you can afford it, and if the new stuff seems plausible for your investigations and research. Keep all of your current equipment in tip top shape by replacing cables, microphones, headphones and the like when it becomes worn or obsolete.

Make a decision early on if you want to be an investigator or a researcher, and there is a big difference. The investigator attempts to find irrefutable paranormal evidence and proof of life after death as does a researcher, but the researcher actually does something with the evidence once it is collected by cataloging and sharing with other top researchers conducting experiments on this topic.

Don't start inventing ways to hoax the scientific community, you will be found out very quickly and any real evidence you submit will be passed off as tainted no matter how great or genuine it is. Conduct and submit your research professionally, methodically and with complete honesty. You will get further in this field with your collected evidence, and easily attain oceans of help and knowledge from credited scientific sources.

Earlier I said that I gave up on the white, pink, brown and crowd noise backgrounds but it just might work for you. I had no success with any of them. I tried them for what seemed to be weeks. I do meditate, pray and play the same soft music at the appropriate time each and every day that I do sessions. I am relaxed and confident with my methods and routine. If something or someone has interrupted my time schedule or if I am in an awkward mood, I cancel the experiment. I do not want the spirits to feel uncomfortable with me or sense my frustration; it is all about trust with them.

I begin with turning on the recording equipment, and inserting a fresh new cassette tape, entering the tape side and number and the machines counter numbers in my daily EVP session journal. I check all of the electronic equipment in the room to make sure it is all up and running. I go over the settings I have written down to make sure that I or the grandkids have not changed anything, unknowingly of course. I begin recording, waiting a full 15 seconds before starting in with my dialog. The microphone is on my desktop and about two feet away from my face. If your microphone has an on/off switch, be sure you check it before you begin. I used my general written dialog and the following is an entry of an EVP session that was conducted on October 28th of 2009 and comes directly from my lab call and response journal. This is exactly how it is written in my log and shows the answers from Margret "Belle" Hayden Prentiss in light grey and marked A.

EVP CALL & RESPONSE SHEET #1

October 28, 2009

It is Wednesday, October 28th, 2009 at 8:02 am. My name is John Douglas Gruber. I am here today to talk to anyone who will speak to me from the other side. I am not here to hurt you in anyway; in fact, I have nothing here that could harm you. All of the gadgets you see me use here are to help me listen and understand you. You can speak freely, without any worry of harm or traps. I will not attempt to make you cross over to the other side. You could simply speak into this box (I point at the microphone here), and I can hear what you have to say. Please, if there is anyone listening to the sound of my voice, respond to me. Give me a sign that you can hear me. May I ask you some questions? (I pause here for 10 seconds) You do not have to answer any question that makes you feel uncomfortable.

Q: Is there anyone in this room with me right now?

A: I am here

Q: Are you willing to speak with me today?

A: Yes

Q: If you can't speak to me, could you move something or make a noise?

A: (No response but, the rusty bell begins to ring)

Q: If you knock on something, let's use once for yes and twice for no, O.K?

A: (No response)

Q: Can you hear me very well?

A: Yes, Yes

Q: Are you male?

A: (No response)

Q: Are you female?

A: Of course I am

Q: Do you know who I am?

A: Yes, I know you

Q: Are there more people here than just you and I?

A: No one else right now

Q: What is your name?

A: You know who I am, I'm Margret

Q: What year is it?

A: 1946, I think…isn't it?

Q: How old are you?

A: 34 I am

Q: Did you live in Columbus, Ohio?

A: Oh yes, I do

Q: Did you work around here?

A: No, I do not work

Q: Have you ever lived in this house?

A: I don't believe so

Q: Were you in the Military?

A: Never

Q: Do you know anyone around here?

A: Just my family

Q: Do you have any family with you?

A: Many others, many

Q: Is there a message that you want me to deliver to someone?

A: Of course! Just to you, you must talk with me

Q: Are you happy where you are right now?

A: I am not

Q: Are there any other family members you wish me to talk with?

A: No, you should stay away from them

Q: Have you talked with your relatives or friends?

A: Many times

Q: Have you crossed over to the other side already?

A: No, but...I want to

Q: Is it beautiful where you are?

A: No, it is not. It's so dark and cold

Q: Are there many others where you are?

A: Oh yes

Q: Is anyone else willing to talk with us today?

A: No

Q: Have you ever talked with someone in this manner before?

A: No, never

Q: Does it make you tired to talk with me?

A: I'm really not sure, a little

Q: May I talk with you again, sometime?

A: Yes, I wish for this

Q: May I take pictures of you the next time we meet?

A: You have already

Q: Thank you for your time, and good day to you.

A: I hope to see you soon Kenneth, very soon

F: End this E.V.P. session at 8:13 am.

After reviewing this recording I decided to use a specific set of questions instead of the general EVP dialog for the next day's session. I now know who I am communicating with and I had specific questions I wanted answered. There was no reason for me to keep asking the same questions over and over each day, I had gotten intelligent responses and I needed to let her know I could hear her and wanted to find out what other information I could obtain. I set down that evening and came up with what I considered important, pertinent questions for the next morning's dialog. I previously had an encounter with Margret at the mausoleum where she was buried. She is in fact the chilling picture on the cover of this book. It had been taken at the Hayden mausoleum about four days before I caught her voice on a recording. I have several more pictures of her and this is why she stated "you all ready have" when I asked the question, "May I take pictures of you the next time we meet?" She also made a reference that she already knew who I was; I can only assume this is because of the earlier encounter in the cemetery. As you may notice she also called me Kenneth in her response to the last question, even after I stated in the beginning I was John D. Gruber. This was very convincing since my birth name was Kenneth and changed to John in my adoption proceedings. This structure is in a great many books as being a "must see" haunted place in Ohio, stating that if you knock three times someone or something always knocks back. Also there is supposed to be a small male child to the right of the big metal doors at the entrance, weeping softly. We gathered no evidence of a small child, and we did not get any knocking response on the entrance doors. We did however, get a few really great pictures and I guess we created a kind of bond with her. We did take hand held recorders to take EVP's that day but, we got what sounds to be a faint chanting in a language we could not understand when we placed it between the doors and a about a foot into the entrance.

You will also take note that she conveyed the desire to cross over into the light and as I have stated many times in this book, I will find out a way to get that done for her. In the few days to follow, I wrote specific dialog sheets to conform to what her answers were to the previous day's questions. I wanted to get as much information to help her, and to find out as much as I could about her present state and situation. I also wanted to know if there is anything evil about where she was and if anything or anyone was holding her there. The chanting sounded kind of evil to some of us, but didn't give us a bad feeling or cause for concern at the time they were recorded. I wrote questions pertaining to the stories of the male child, and to a secret society that her husband and father were allegedly members of for many years when they were alive. Armed with all of this background, stories and history in my mind, and taking in consideration what she had already told me, I scribbled out my next specific questions. I left a printed copy of the questions on the desk top overnight just in case she could see them in advance. I had no idea whether she was speaking to me directly from the cemetery or from inside my lab. All of my friends and fellow researchers cautioned me that she could be some kind of siren or temptress just setting me up for a big fall, so I proceeded with care and kept a level head. This was the most exciting few days I had ever encountered, but I didn't rush as I have been told that time is but a fleeting second to spirits which I pretty much believe now since she thinks it is 1946 and she passed away in 1939. She also thought she was 34 years old yet she was over 70 when she slipped away. The following was my next day's dialog and Margret's answers, again her answers are in grey.

EVP CALL & RESPONSE SHEET #2

October 29th, 2009

It is (Thursday, October 29, 2009 @07:58:04 am). My name is John Douglas Gruber; you may know me as Kenneth. I am here today to talk to Margret only. I am not here to hurt you Margret in anyway; in fact, I have nothing here that could harm you. All of the gadgets you see me use here are to help me listen and understand you. You can speak freely, without any worry of harm or traps from me. I will not attempt to make you cross over to the other side today. You could simply speak into this box (I point at microphone here), and I can hear what you have to say. Please, if you are listening to the sound of my voice, respond to me. Give me a sign that you can hear me. Margret or "Belle" Hayden Prentiss please come through to me. I have more questions for you. Again, you do not have to answer any question that makes you feel uncomfortable.

Q: Margret, are you in this room with me right now?

A: Yes, I am here.

Q: Are you willing & can you speak freely with me today?

A: Yes, I can.

Q: If you can't speak to me, could you move something or make a noise?

A: (No response)

Q: If you knock on something, let's use once for yes and twice for no, O.K.?

A: (No response)

Q: Can you hear my voice very well?

A: Yes, yes I can hear you.

Q: Did you try to get my attention before by moving a bell in this room?

A: Oh yes! ...This one. (The rusty bell moves and dings once, softly)

Q: Are there more people here than just you and I right now?

A: No, not right now.

Q: How many spirits are with you in this place?

A: All of us.

Q: Who is with you right now?

A: I'm alone now.

Q: You want us to stay away from the rest of your family...Why Margret?

A: Just my father Charles and husband, Frederick.

Q: Is there Evil in that Mausoleum, can it hurt us?

A: They think they can...but, I know better.

Q: Does it have something to do with the dark secret society?

A: Yes, they can't hold it open ...the water is gone!

Q: Are you being held in that cold, dark place against your will?

A: It's getting better ...but, yes.

Q: If you are, can you tell me who is keeping you here?

A: Yes, Frederick and Daddy.

Q: Is anybody else being held against their will?

A: Yes, more are.

Q: You said you wanted to cross over, do you need our help?

A: Yes, we want your help...we need your help.

Q: Are there others that wish to cross over to the light with you?

A: Yes...three of us.

Q: If there is anyone else who are they... what are their names?

A: Marie...Lillian...and I.

Q: Are any of these spirits your children?

A: There are no children here...none.

Q: You seem to appear naked to us in our pictures…why Margret?

A: I am being punished, n'…I am so sorry, and ashamed.

Q: Are you tired or afraid to talk with me?

A: No…I am not afraid.

Q: Please…may I talk with you again, tomorrow?

A: I will talk to you as long as I can.

Q: Is it alright to have others speak to you?

A: I do not wish to speak to anyone else…they cannot help me!

Q: Thank you for speaking with me today…I will help you Margret!

A: I must go now! …I must leave! …I must hurry!

F: End this EVP session at 08:09:52 am.

As you can see, I changed the introduction to fit Margret, and to attempt to speak to only her. By the sixth question she was moving the rusty bell again, very softly and it seemed effortlessly. I wanted to make sure that nobody evil was listening to our conversation and I hit that point very strong in several questions. I was able to ascertain that she and at least two others were in fact being held against their will. Her husband Frederick and father Charles had conveyed to her she was a bad person and could not leave the mausoleum for any reason and that someone was the punisher for her mortal sins. What intrigued me the most I guess, was this water she kept referring to. There was no water in the front of the mausoleum, a medium sized water hole commonly called "the pit" was behind and not missing or gone, and the item we found most unsettling was a baptismal font in the middle of the crypts. What possible reason would that item be in a cemetery let alone in a mausoleum? And what door was she referring to? The door on the entrance to the crypt was log chained with a big padlock on it. I established that she trusted me enough to talk to me as long as she was able to, and I felt comfortable with the conversations as well. It seemed that something on her end interrupted the session just as it was about to close when she stated that she must leave in a hurry, so for the next session I will have to find out why. After reviewing and cataloging all of this information, I took on the task of writing down the next day's questions. I had to keep in mind that I only wanted to ask between twenty or thirty of them as I noticed her voice would become weaker as the session came closer to the end. I also looked up more history and went to the Columbus Metropolitan Library's historical employees on the second floor. They were great and got into it and were excited about the research as much if not more than I. We discovered there was a reflecting pond in front of the mausoleum many years ago, but we could not discern what year it was filled in. Could this have been the water Margret was speaking of? Did it hold some kind of life giving power to the inhabitants inside? Paranormal events and spirits have always been known to be drawn or at least linked to water and lime stone laden areas. This particular area had the best of both worlds; with the small lake of water and the bottom full of limestone it is no wonder why this site was a prime spot for any kind of paranormal activity.

The next set of dialog for tomorrow's session had to be even more in depth than any of the previous ones. I want to make sure she was not afraid to talk with me and to assure her and the others that I would attempt to help them cross over into the light. I also needed to find out who had handed down her punishment or judgment and yet, make sure she was not tricking me into something bad. I wanted to get to the bottom of what energy they used and how did they replenish it, by what source did the supply come from. I needed to get to the chanting we all thought we heard in the early "on site" recordings, to find out who, what, and why the possible chant was being said and in what language. I wanted to work in some questions about that door she refers to that somebody wants to keep open, and why. Is it an evil portal, or something good they are using to help cross spirits? Well, I soon found out more than I wanted to. The following is the EVP session logged for Friday, October 30th, 2009; her answers are again printed in a light grey font.

EVP CALL & RESPONSE SHEET #3

October 30th, 2009

It is (Friday, October 30, 2009 @ 08:02:06 am) my name is John Douglas Gruber; you may know me as Kenneth. I am here today to talk to Margret only. I am not here to hurt you Margret in anyway; in fact, I have nothing here that could harm you. All of the gadgets you see me use here are to help me listen and understand you. You can speak freely, without any worry of harm or traps from me. I will not attempt to make you cross over to the other side today. You could simply speak into this box (point at mic here), and I can hear what you have to say. Please, if you are listening to the sound of my voice, respond to me. Give me a sign that you can hear me. Margret or "Belle" Hayden Prentiss please come through to me again. I have more questions for you. You do not have to answer any question that makes you feel uncomfortable.

Q: Margret, are you here with me today?

A: Yes, I am here.

Q: Are you willing to speak with me today?

A: Yes, of course.

Q: Can you hear my voice very well?

A: Oh yes.

Q: Are there more people here than just you and I right now?

A: No, there are not.

Q: Is there anybody else listening to us right now?

A: No, no.

Q: Is there is someone listening, is it safe for you to talk to me?

A: It is safe now.

Q: I do not want to cause you any danger?

A: You are not.

Q: Please do not get upset with this question, but are you trying to trick me or to hurt me in any way?

A: Oh no, no, please…no!

Q: Margret, I give you my word that we will try and help you and your family move into the light.

A: This is great, thank you so much.

Q: Can you personally leave the Mausoleum grounds?

A: No, I think I may not.

Q: Who has set your boundaries, if you have any?

A: I have been told that GOD has set my place.

Q: Have you shown yourself to other people from the steps of the Mausoleum?

A: No, only that one time.

Q: What "water", are you speaking of?

A: The reflecting lake out front…it is gone.

Q: Have you ever tried to cross over to the light?

A: Many times, but I need help.

Q: Does it take a lot of your energy to show yourself to us?

A: Oh my yes…way too much.

Q: Does it take a lot of energy to speak with us?

A: Yes, yes it does.

Q: How do you replenish your energy?

A: From the sun, and air…and visitors.

Q: Is there some way I can help you with your energy?

A: No, I would make you tired…sleepy.

Q: How do Frederick and Charles get the energy they need?

A: The same way, visitors...the sun.

Q: Do you know there is a chant being recited in the Mausoleum?

A: Yes, it is annoying, it, it is nuts.

Q: Why is somebody chanting in the Mausoleum?

A: It holds open the door.

Q: Who is chanting, and what are their names?

A: Harry, Frederick, Peter, Daisy and Daddy.

Q: Can you tell me what language the chant is being recited in?

A: Imperial Aramaic...I believe.

Q: Is it some kind of Evil chant?

A: It keeps the door open, but it is weak. It is closing fast. It is not good.

Q: Can you explain to me what the chant means?

A: I must leave now! It is not safe for us! I must leave, I must go quickly! I will talk again.

Q: Can you tell me what is being said in the chant?

A: (No response)

Q: Does the chanting ever stop?

A: (No response)

Q: Please, may I talk with you again, tomorrow?

A: (No response)

Q: Thank you for speaking with me again today, I will help you Margret!

A: (No response)

 F: End this EVP session at 08:12:04 am

Well in this session I accomplished a lot. I found that it was safe to talk with her during this session and she was not in any danger for the moment. I informed her that I would be getting the proper people to help her and the others cross over into the light as soon as I could. It is now established where she and the other inhabitants get there energy, she affirmed the water source.

My questions lead me to the answers of how much energy is used in communicating with me, thus the fading off toward the end of our conversations was explained, and how she replenished it. She gave me great clues as to the language used in the faint chant we had previously recorded, but gave no information as to what was being said. The door she kept referring to is still was up in the air. Through later conversations during sessions I found that the other spirits were allegedly trying to keep a door or portal open for the addition of more members. The door they tried to keep open for so long was closing because the water from the lake was gone and had been filled in. She again cut this session short for whatever reason. It became very clear that she needed to be crossed over very soon.

The sessions lasted three more days in which I gave her instructions to give us a small sign only to spare her energy when we were ready at the mausoleum to begin the crossing over task. I also told her to not wait for anybody else; the three of them should run into the light as soon as they could see it. We would deal with any stragglers after we knew for sure she was finally safe and gone.

It was a beautiful Sunday morning and Linda, Jacquie, Jacob, Phillip, Robin, Mathew, Helen, Father Martin, other SPATS members and I went to the site and began praying and calling Margret to come out and cross armed with Holy Water and many scriptures. We all turned around at the same time toward my car that was parked very close because we heard a tapping noise, like someone tapping on the windshield and we decided that this was our sign that they were present. We all filled the area with white light and kept praying. The strangest thing we all noticed right off was the lack of any movement, there was not a sound, not a bird, no wind just completely quiet and calm. The hair stood up on all of us as we kept on saying our prayers for the crossing over event, some of us got very emotional and began to weep. The air was very heavy which made it a little difficult to breath at times.

First a very large black bird, we think it was a crow darted out of a huge tree from out in front of the mausoleum and flew very quickly out of site. Then three other large black birds just showed up, we have no idea where they came from. The three circled right above us for about two to three minutes not making a sound, then took off in the same direction as the first. It then came to us that it was very quiet and calm again, no wind, no other animals to be heard. We stayed the course with our prayers, but kept a watchful eye on our surroundings.

The step area to the entrance had always been about 20° to 30° colder, it was hard to tell if this was due to the fact that they were marble steps which holds its own temperature, or from something else. This spot had now become as warm as the rest of the surrounding areas, leaving us to believe that the original cold temps we had recorded several times earlier were not due to the marble steps, but to something paranormal. The psychic present stated everybody that wanted to cross had done so, and all of us took note that birds started flying around and singing like it was just another normal day, as if nothing happened. The air was lighter, a breeze kicked up and everybody seemed to be comfortable and back to normal as far as emotions and senses. We got no more readings from our EMF, K2 and EVP equipment what so ever.

I have not had communication with Margret "Belle" Hayden Prentiss since that day. Oh I have tried to no avail, but I was pleased with what we accomplished and what evidence and information we had obtained from the whole ordeal. This was the event of a lifetime for me, and if I stopped right now with my research I would still feel very proud of my accomplishments. It was very rewarding to have been a part of this spirit rescue and I will never forget it. And just imagine, it all started with doing EVP's in my home office and ended up being the greatest adventure I have ever been a part of. And by the way, thank you to all that participated in this endeavor, you're the best.

Chapter Ten: 10

Final Thoughts

Ok, let's recap all of the information we have been over. Make sure the area of expertise you choose fits your budget and your personality. Field work is more for the go getter while the home lab is for the laid back comfortable personality. Equipment can get very expensive if you let it, however there are great deals to be had on the internet auction blocks. You do not need to have the most ultimate and expensive equipment out there to be an investigator or researcher and gather great paranormal evidence. You can start out with good and progress to better then best, always reselling the lower quality equipment to recoup some of the laid out money. Or, who knows, you might not even like being a paranormal field investigator. The money is null and the hours upon hours of analysis is exhausting. Lugging equipment and setting it up is a major chore. Looking for a well established field group or starting your own from scratch can be a very slow and expensive endeavor. Just getting your name out to let people know you even exist can be very costly with website fees and local newspaper ads. Finding a great group of people to investigate with that doesn't leave pizza boxes and beer cans for the caretaker to clean up and personalities that fit yours can be hard to find. You may never get to purchase the best equipment and just give up because investigating may not be your thing. You also might love it and end up doing it for years to come, and be the one that gathers the proof positive that the world is waiting and aching for.

Home based paranormal EVP research is my passion, it cost about the same as field work but I don't have to lug stuff around, advertise or even look for anybody else to help me do my thing, and yes, I can eat pizza.

Whichever path you choose in the paranormal research world, should go through as much information on the topic as you can, become a vacuum cleaner of sorts and take it all in. Come up with your own tactics, methods and plans of attack after wading through the good, the bad and the BS you will read from all the resources you can find. Make sure you hit the history of EVP articles and resources to find out methods others have tried and what worked and what didn't.

Formulate your game plan early, this gives you time to review and revise if you need to. Make sure that you are confident in the delivery of your intro and questions, and always be sincere and have compassion. Get into a routine that will fit your time frames and will be compatible with your lifestyle. If you use music to alert the spirits you are about to begin, pick something you like to hear as well, something current if you're not going to use shanghai, but not wild and head banging. Meditation and prayer is a tool that many use before their EVP sessions. Leave the questions on your desk over night in plain view, and light candles if you want to just before and during your sessions. No matter what questions and methods you use, rehearse them until you become flawless, and don't forget to give time between questions for the spirits to form answers.

Know your equipment! Practice recording, downloading, and analyzing the kids, a radio, the T.V. even your dog barking on your equipment set up. You have to become very familiar with the proper way to get the best recording and to avoid equipment failure during a session. Check all of the power connections and patch cords to insure a proper download to your computer. Use the filters on the software to remove pops and room noise. Get use to reducing hiss with noise reduction tools from within the software. Learn how to reduce the chance of over filtration with your particular brand of software, although it will happen. Set up mock files on your computer as initial tests to insure you are getting it right, and don't touch the RAW file.

As far as recording goes, play with the volume controls on the mixing board and the recorder. Jot down your settings just in case they get moved or accidently adjusted. Always remember to put the headphones in to the recorder jack not the soundboard. You will want to know what you are recording, not the great sound the recorder is possibly missing.

Send your great evidence to proper research people for authentication and make sure you catalog all of your hard work in your journals. Keep in mind you should also keep record of the way you caught the evidence for your future reference.

For field work, make sure you get well acquainted with all of your equipment and instruments. Be friendly and professional toward all your clients and above all, don't leave a mess for them to clean up. You want them to be glad they called you for the job, not regretful that you are there.

Remember to help spirits if they ask for it, and never use trickery or falsify your results. Credibility is essential to the world of paranormal evidence and research. There are many people who already think that this field is line of crap, let's not add to it. Be open with your clients in field work, they will be more honest and forth coming to you if they know you are sincere and passionate with their situation.

Above all, have fun. If you choose either of these paranormal avenues, fun and rewards await. It is what you make it. You can find a great bunch of field investigators to hang around and have the time of your life learning and researching the most controversial topic of our new age. I have had the best time recording and capturing EVP's over all of the other hobbies I have ever tried. It is both fun and gratifying.

You will go from down to up in this research in a split second, never doubt that. I have had periods of complete frustration to total elation in a matter of just days. You never know what is out there waiting for you, wanting you to communicate with them, or at the least, wanting to let you know they're here.

I hope that this book and my insight will help you in your trek for the truth. Folks, it is out there, it is real and it is nothing short of miraculous. When you get your first class "A" EVP, I wish I could be a fly on the wall. You will be so excited you will hardly contain yourself. I love this hobby and will continue it till I can no longer do it. You will meet spirits from all walks of life, with all kinds of messages, and all types of emotions. You will even get voices from beyond when you least expect it. I have often caught myself saying, "I know I didn't get anything because it was just another routine day". In fact some of the best evidence I have captured came from just such a day.

I use to keep my research hidden from the public and locals, but I have found that every time I talk about it with a group of people somebody recalls a story of paranormal experience and then the whole dam room starts coming forth with stories. So I feel that it is time to wake up and start paying attention to what people have to say and learning from their tales. Test this theory for yourself. In a gathering of a few friends, start talking about something odd that happened to you that could not be explained and you will soon be sitting back and watching the room snowball into the best paranormal conversation ever. And it is very fascinating to me that this experiment has worked everywhere I go. Even with people I hardly know.

The spirits will do this, too. Soon your lab or office will be the gateway to our side and communication will become abundant for you. The word will spread and you will never lack for a spirit or two to talk with. Friends are captivated with the evidence I have collected over the years. I am not trying to break any records, and I do have a regular life. I do stick to my routine every day that I am home, but I do not give up living my life either. So I guess that this is my warning to you, don't let this become an OCD (obsessive compulsive disorder) that takes over your every waking moment. You might think I am nuts, but there are those that can't stop doing this.

It is a thrill but to do 15 or 20 sessions a day is what I would call over kill. Most of the sprits that have contacted me through my methods have been gone quite a long time, so I don't see any rush to communicate with them that often. I am told that 20 years is nothing but a blink of an eye to the spirits anyway, so what is another day compared to that.

And as far as demons go, a researcher or investigator could do his work for over 40 years and never encounter even the first one. Just remember if you have opened the door for spirits to communicate with you today, close that door when you are finished with it today and you will never get any goofball spirits invading your lab or office.

Have fun with this and I hope you will get great results as I feel I have. Send me your lab pictures and your cool collected voices if you want to. I always enjoy seeing and hearing stories of research success. Let me know if something is working very well for you, and tell me what you have tried that wasn't so hot.

Remember, we are all in this world together so let's share ideas. Keep in mind I never post any evidence on our website but I will give you feedback on what you send me. And I am always glad to answer or find an answer to any questions you might have about this wonderful topic. You should also reach out to some really great people on the internet; many organizations are willing to answer your questions and share your ideas as long as you are sincere.

Happy hunting and I hope to hear from you.

John D. Gruber Ph.D.

Appendix A

Figure 01

Hereward Carrington, Ph.D. (born Hubert Lavington) (17 October 1880 – 26 December 1958) was a well-known British investigator of psychic phenomena and author. His subjects included several of the most high-profile cases of apparent psychic ability of his times, and he wrote over 100 books on subjects including the paranormal and psychical research, conjuring and stage magic and alternative health issues.

Figure 02

Thomas Alva Edison (February 11, 1847 – October 18, 1931) was an American inventor, scientist and businessman who developed many devices that greatly influenced life around the world, including the phonograph, the motion picture camera, and a long-lasting, practical electric light bulb. Dubbed "The Wizard of Menlo Park" (now Edison, New Jersey) by a newspaper reporter, he was one of the first inventors to apply the principles of mass production and large teamwork to the process of invention, and therefore is often credited with the creation of the first industrial research laboratory.

Edison is considered one of the most prolific inventors in history, holding 1,093 U.S. patents in his name, as well as many patents in the United Kingdom, France and Germany. He is credited with numerous inventions that contributed to mass communication and, in particular, telecommunications. His advanced work in these fields was an outgrowth of his early career as a telegraph operator. Edison originated the concept and implementation of electric-power generation and distribution to homes, businesses, and factories – a crucial development in the modern industrialized world. His first power station was on Manhattan Island, New York.

Figure 03

Raymond Bayless, the extraordinary claimed phenomenon of telephone calls from the dead, one of a variety of new forms of contact with the dead using modern technology was raised by parapsychologists D. Scott Rogo and Raymond Bayless in their 1979 book Phone Calls from the Dead. Their research had been stimulated by a report in the September 1976 Fate Magazine from Don B. Owens of Toledo, Ohio, concerning his close friend Lee Epps. They had lived in the same neighborhood for years before Lee moved away and their contact became limited to occasional meetings or telephone calls. Raymond Bayless Author of many books such as: Experiences of a Psychical Researcher, Phone Calls from the Dead, Voices from Beyond, The Journal of the Southern California Society for Psychical Research Volume 2, Apparitions and Survival of Death, The enigma of the Poltergeist, The Exorcism Series Set of 8 Books, and The Other Side of Death.

Figure 04

Friedrich Jürgenson was born in Odessa in 1903. His mother was Swedish, and his father of Danish descent. The family had moved to Odessa from Estonia, and the father was a physician. Jürgenson trained as a painter at the Art Academy and as a singer and musician at the Odessa Conservatory. The family moved back to Estonia in 1925, and Friedrich Jürgenson moved on to Berlin to further his studies. 1932 he moved to Palestine with his tutor, the bass singer Tito Scipa, and stayed on for six years. In 1938 he moved to Milan for studies as well as performances. By way of Estonia, where he visited his parents in 1943, he came to Sweden, where he married and became a Swedish citizen. He sustained himself and his wife by painting portraits of the well-to-do. When he was in Italy and Pompeii in 1949, he was recognized by the Vatican, which promptly employed him to have its archeological treasures cataloged. The Vatican was so impressed by his work, that the Pope, Pius XII, ordered a portrait of himself by Jürgenson. Finally a total of four portraits were painted.

Then in 1957, when tape recorders were already commonplace, Jürgenson acquired one to record his singing, but soon enough he began to notice strange phenomena on his tapes, but at that stage mostly unexplainable fade-ins and fade-outs. Then he started to sense telepathic messages, but inside of himself – not on the tapes. In 1959 he brought his tape recorder along to the family's summer cottage to record birds. When he played back the tape it was saturated with hiss and noise, and he could barely detect the bird song inside it all. Suddenly, in the midst of the noise, a trumpet-like signal interrupted the hiss, and the startled Jürgenson heard a voice speaking in Norwegian! Right after that the tape functioned normally, reproducing all the sounds of the birds that it had been his intent to record.

Figure 05

Dr. Konstantīns Raudive (1909–1974) was a Latvian writer and intellectual, and husband of Zenta Mauriņa. Raudive was born in Latvia but studied extensively abroad, later becoming a student of Carl Jung.[1] In exile following the Soviet re-conquest of Latvia in World War II, he taught at the University of Uppsala in Sweden. Raudive studied parapsychology all his life, and was especially interested in the possibility of the afterlife. He and German parapsychologist Hans Bender investigated Electronic Voice Phenomena (EVP). He published a book on EVP, Breakthrough in 1971. Raudive was a scientist as well as a practicing Roman Catholic. In 1964, Raudive read Friedrich Jürgenson's book, Voices from Space, and was so impressed by it that he arranged to meet Jürgenson in 1965. He then worked with Jürgenson to make some EVP recordings, but their first efforts bore little fruit, although they believed that they could hear very weak, muddled voices. According to Raudive, however, one night, as he listened to one recording, he clearly heard a number of voices. When he played the tape over and over, he came to believe he understood all of them. He thought some of which were in German, some in Latvian, some in French. The last voice on the tape, according to Raudive, a woman's voice, said "Va dormir, Margarete" ("Go to sleep, Margaret").

Raudive later wrote (in his book Breakthrough): "These words made a deep impression on me, as Margarete Petrautzki had died recently, and her illness and death had greatly affected me."

Figure 06

George W. Meek was a retired industrialist who had revolutionized the air-conditioning industry and had made a small fortune on a series of patents. With a commanding presence at six-foot-three, he possessed a powerful intentionality that was apparent whether watching him march straight to the podium for a speech or whether observing him quickly chunk down a complex research project into tasks that he could delegate to his staff. Like all men of good character, George had learned to still that little inner voice that advocates bad choices from day to day, until the voice had become weak and ineffective. He had learned to make the right choices again and again until they had become habit. Over the years his intentionality had shaped a comfortable and pleasant lifestyle for his family. It had also spurred the creation of the Metascience Foundation, Meek's highly regarded, nonprofit enterprise to analyze the human spirit from a scientific angle. Meek spent many hours in his large basement office piecing together roadmaps of the spirit worlds from the vast knowledge he had gained from his research. He had discovered that the actual locations of Heaven and Hell were not somewhere out there in distant space nor hidden away deep inside the Earth, but right here, all around us. He knew that mystics over the centuries have had an intimate knowledge of the fact that many universes interpenetrate our own physical universe, but they didn't know how to explain it to the world.

Figure 07

Hans Bender (5 February 1907 – 7 May 1991), (Pictured in the middle with Friedrich Jürgenson) was a German lecturer on the subject of parapsychology, who was also responsible for establishing the parapsychological institute Institut für Grenzgebiete der Psychologie und Psychohygiene in Freiburg. For many years his pipe smoking, contemplative figure was synonymous with German parapsychology. He was an investigator of 'unusual human experience', e.g. poltergeists and clairvoyants. One of his most famous cases was the Rosenheim Poltergeist. He was a German psychologist, parapsychologist and physiologist who wrote on ESP, Psychokinesis, poltergeists, mediums, spontaneous phenomena and spiritual healing. He was married and had three kids. Died of AIDS on 5/07/1991, 11:36 AM MEDT, Freiberg, Germany.

Figure 08

Raymond Cass: Raymond was born in Yorkshire in 1921 and educated at Riley High School in Hull. From an early age he became interested in the Paranormal, reading avidly on the subject. The massive slaughter on the Western Front raised serious questions in his mind about the purpose of life and the futility of war. He was engrossed in Harmsworths 'History of World War 1' when a male voice suddenly called his name over a primitive radio which was switched off at the time. Alone in his grandfathers seafront mansion, this was an enigmatic experience, but even at the age of 7 he was aware of paranormal forces. The primitive horn-like loud speaker could have only been activated by some kind of magnetic pulse or flux. To gain a more intimate knowledge of the paranormal, he joined a Hull psychic society and it was at this point he found that an ancestor, Robert Cass who died in 1898, was not only the founder of spiritualism in Hull but also a powerful medium who could levitate a heavy table with 3 men on top to the ceiling. They wrote their names there with carpenter's pencils. A Psychic thread in his lineage first emerged in 1773 in Leaming, North Yorkshire, where Molly Cass was persecuted as a medium and psychic. In 1938, at a Helen Duncan séance in Bridlington it was predicted that Raymond would develop voice medium ship.

Although it was not until October 1971 and the release of Konstantin Raudive's book, 'Breakthrough', that this prophecy came true and as part of a dedicated team of EVP buffs, Raymond rapidly overtook other UK researchers and produced voices of clarity and amplitude which attracted worldwide attention. He produced examples of the much disputed 'Polyglot' voices where a sentence would contain the elements of various different foreign languages. Fluent in German, Raymond was able to keep up with European experimenters, aided by his association with the German section of the foreign office. But on his release in 1945 from a German prisoner of war camp he was forced to shelve his passion for psychic affairs and concentrate on earning a living. Interested in acoustics, he qualified to trade in hearing aid technology and founded his own practice in Yorkshire where he was active for 20 years. During this time he found the resources to begin experimenting with EVP in association with the well known experimenter Mike Vinter. Raymond Cass was considered one of the 'Worlds' foremost researchers into EVP. His voice samples have been played at many lectures and presentations worldwide. Raymond's tapes have been the focus of study by various institutions such as the Bio-Energetics Institute in Osaka, Japan, The Parapsychology Unit of Olivert College, Michigan, USA, and The ESP Research Associates Foundation at Little Rock, Arkansas and the Parapsychology Unit at Freidburg University. His work has been observed by the War Department, USA and the Ministry of Defense in the UK.

Figure 09

Pope Pius XII, born Eugenio Maria Giuseppe Giovanni Pacelli (2 March 1876 – 9 October 1958), reigned as the 260th Pope, head of the Catholic Church and sovereign of Vatican City State, from 2 March 1939 until his death in 1958.

Before election to the papacy, Pacelli served as secretary of the Department of Extraordinary Ecclesiastical Affairs, papal nuncio and Cardinal Secretary of State, in which capacity he worked to conclude treaties with European and Latin American nations, most notably the Reichskonkordat with Germany. His leadership of the Catholic Church during World War II remains the subject of continued historical controversy.

After the war, Pius XII contributed to the rebuilding of Europe, and advocated peace and reconciliation, including lenient policies toward vanquished nations and the unification of Europe. The Church, flourishing in the West, experienced severe persecution and mass deportations of Catholic clergy in the East. In light of his protests, and his involvement in the Italian elections of 1948, he became known as a staunch opponent of communism. He signed 30 concordats and diplomatic treaties.

Figure 10

Pope Paul VI, born Giovanni Battista Enrico Antonio Maria Montini (26 September 1897 – 6 August 1978), reigned as Pope of the Roman Catholic Church and Sovereign of Vatican City from 1963 to 1978 succeeding Pope John XXIII, who had convened the Second Vatican Council, he decided to continue it. He fostered improved ecumenical relations with Orthodox, Anglicans and Protestants, which resulted in a number of historic meetings and agreements.

Montini served in the Vatican's State Department from 1922 to 1954. While in the State Department, Montini and Domenico Tardini were considered as the closest and most influential co-workers of Pope Pius XII, who named him in 1954 Archbishop of the largest Italian dioceses, Milan, a function which made him automatically Secretary of the Italian Bishops Conference. John XXIII elevated him to the College of Cardinals in 1958, and after his death, Montini was considered the favorite successor.

He took on the name Paul, to indicate a renewed worldwide mission to spread the message of Christ.

Figure 11

In 1982, Sarah Estep founded the American Association of Electronic Voice Phenomena (AA-EVP) in Severna Park, Maryland, a nonprofit organization with the purpose of increasing awareness of EVP, and of teaching standardized methods for capturing it. Estep began her exploration of EVP in 1976, and says she has made hundreds of recordings of messages from deceased friends, relatives, and other individuals, including Konstantin Raudive, Beethoven, a lamplighter from 18th century Philadelphia, Pennsylvania, and extraterrestrials whom she speculated originated from other planets or dimensions.

Figure 12

Sir Oliver Lodge was born in 1851 at Penkhull in Stoke-on-Trent and educated at Adams' Grammar School. He was the eldest of eight sons and a daughter of Oliver Lodge (1826–1884) Lodge obtained a Bachelor of Science degree from the University of London in 1875 and a Doctor of Science in 1877. He was appointed professor of physics and mathematics at University College, Liverpool in 1881. In 1900 Lodge moved from Liverpool back to the Midlands and became the first principal of the new Birmingham University, remaining there until his retirement in 1919.

Figure 13

D. Scott Rogo (February 1, 1950—August 18, 1990) was a writer and researcher on subjects related to parapsychology. He wrote or co-wrote 20 books and more than 100 magazine and journal articles, 7 books were reprinted in 2005 by Anomalist books', leaving the body was reprinted in 2008 by Simon & Schuster. Rogo was active at the Psychical Research Foundation (formerly at Durham, North Carolina) and at Maimonides Medical Center in Brooklyn, New York. The D. Scott Rogo Award was established in 1992 to benefit authors working on manuscripts pertaining to parapsychology.

Born in Los Angeles, California and educated at the University of Cincinnati and San Fernando Valley State College (now California State University, Northridge; he graduated summa cum laude from the latter institution in 1972. (His B.A. was in music; Rogo played the oboe and the English horn, and for two years played professionally with the San Diego Symphony and other ensembles.) Rogo served as a consulting editor for Fate Magazine for which he wrote a regular column; he advocated greater involvement by both researchers and skeptics in parapsychological research. He was killed during a break-in at his apartment in Northridge, California on August 14, 1990.

Figure 14

In 1980, William O'Neil constructed an electronic audio device called "The Spiricom." O'Neil claimed the device was built to specifications which he received psychically from George Mueller, a scientist who had died six years previously. At a Washington, DC, press conference on April 6, 1982, O'Neil stated that he was able to hold two-way conversations with spirits through the Spiricom device, and provided the design specifications to researchers for free. However, nobody is known to have replicated O'Neil's results using their own Spiricom devices. O'Neil's partner, retired industrialist George Meek, attributed O'Neil's success, and the inability of others to replicate it, to O'Neil's mediumistic abilities forming part of the loop that made the system work. However, there is strong evidence to suggest that the recordings of conversations were falsified by O'Neil, specifically with an electrolarynx. The clearly audible vocal fricatives in the recordings, along with the facts that during the hours of recordings

O'Neil's and Mueller's voices never overlaps (as would happen in normal conversation), support this theory.

Figure 15

G. Gilbert Bonner (1924 – 1997)

George Gilbert Bonner studied the Electronic Voice Phenomenon for over 20 years. He started researching EVP when he was in his mid 40's. As a psychologist and artist George subjectively approached the EVP with great passion. Gilbert issued a tape as he approached 65 to his colleagues and friends.

As a psychotherapist he knew the power of the mind yet at no stage did he ever doubt the voices on the tape. Paranormal voices can be demonstrated by voice print analysis that identifies both male and female with their individual characteristics clearly charted. But in listening tests spanning over several years Bonner could hear the same voice coming through countless times on his tapes. Bonner also points out, when a voice is captured on a tape and can be played over and over again this cannot be halucinary voices.

Bonner (as did Cass) had contact with Meek, Estep, Sherman and many more researchers of the time. He also wrote to Jurgensen who ignored his mail (as he did with most people).As with many of the great EVP researchers, Bonner had no interest in psychic activity or the paranormal until he had listened to the Raudive tapes and captured voices himself. He worked 7 days a week and was once called a 'Voice Hunter'. Bonner tried for over a year to get a 'Spiricom' device up and working but had no luck at all getting a voice to come through. He believed that the voices where the closest thing he had ever come across as evidence of survival after death.

Bonner wrote or worked for the SPR, a US Military base, Fate Magazine, plus many foreign magazines. George allegedly had over 50000 examples.

Figure 16

Sir Arthur Ignatius Conan Doyle, DL (22 May 1859 – 7 July 1930) was a Scottish physician and writer, most noted for his stories about the detective Sherlock Holmes, which are generally considered a major innovation in the field of crime fiction, and for the adventures of Professor Challenger. He was a prolific writer whose other works include science fiction stories, historical novels, plays and romances, poetry, and non-fiction. Arthur Conan Doyle was born on 22 May 1859 in Edinburgh, Scotland, to an English father of Irish descent, Charles Altamont Doyle, and an Irish mother, née Mary Foley. His parents were married in 1855.

Although he is now referred to as "Conan Doyle", the origin of this compound surname (if that is how he meant it to be understood) is uncertain. The entry in which his baptism is recorded in the register of St Mary's Cathedral in Edinburgh gives 'Arthur Ignatius Conan' as his Christian name, and the simple 'Doyle' as his surname. It also names Michael Conan as his godfather.

Conan Doyle was sent to the Roman Catholic Jesuit preparatory school Hodder Place, Stonyhurst, at the age of nine. He then went on to Stonyhurst College, but by the time he left the school in 1875, he had rejected Christianity to become an agnostic.

Conan Doyle was friends for a time with the American magician Harry Houdini, who himself became a prominent opponent of the Spiritualist movement in the 1920s following the death of his beloved mother. Although Houdini insisted that Spiritualist mediums employed trickery (and consistently attempted to expose them as frauds), Conan Doyle became convinced that Houdini himself possessed supernatural powers, a view expressed in Conan Doyle's The Edge of the Unknown. Houdini was apparently unable to convince Conan Doyle that his feats were simply illusions, leading to a bitter public falling out between the two.

All of the information in this book about past and present researchers of EVP and their pictures, different methods and opinions of EVP research other than mine, and EVP software were obtained by several different web sites and are not my thoughts or in any way my own original writings. A list of the informational sites, excerpts, and pictures are as follows:

Wikipedia, the Free Encyclopedia
EVP Research Association UK (the EVP Timeline)
The Raymond Cass Foundation
AAEVP.com
Crucible.org
Insight Paranormal Inc
Ehow.com

Appendix B
Research sites, articles and books

The following websites I found were very worth the time for more information on procedures and methods of successfully collecting EVP evidence. They are in alphabetical order.

Web Sites

http://en.wikipedia.org/wiki/Electronic_voice_phenomenon

http://evpinformation.com/

http://flamelcollege.org/

http://ghostpix.com/index-5EVP.htm

http://paranormalsciences.com/rich_text_1.html

http://the-atlantic-paranormal-society.com/articles/technical/whitenoise.html

http://theshadowlands.net/ghostwav.htm

http://www.aaevp.com/

http://www.altereddimensions.net/ghosts/evp.aspx

http://www.assap.org/newsite/htmlfiles/Recording%20EVP.html

http://www.bellaonline.com/articles/art42238.asp

http://www.crucible.org/equip_paranormal.htm

http://www.evpuk.com/evp_equipment.html

http://www.ghostpix.com/recordingevp.html

http://www.ghoststudy.com/new6/article_submissions/evp.htm

http://www.ghostweb.com/evp_how.html

http://www.haunted-places.com/

http://www.mcmsys.com/~brammer/evpfilepage2.htm

http://www.paranormalghost.com/evp_software_analysis.htm

http://www.prairieghosts.com/voice.html

http://www.trueghosttales.com/evp.php

Books

✓ **There Is No Death and There Are No Dead** (Paperback)
Written by Tom W. Butler (Author), Lisa F. Butler (Author)

✓ **Speak with the Dead: Seven Methods for Spirit Communication**
(Paperback) by Konstantinos (Author)

✓ **THE ELECTRONIC GHOSTS: EVP** (electronic voice phenomenon)
(Paperback) by NATHAN TOMS (Author)

Evp: Electronic Voice Phenomenon: Massachusetts Ghostly Voices
(Paperback) by Mike Markowicz (Author)

✓ **How to Record & Analyze EVP Voices on Your Home Computer** (with
CD) http://www.hauntedplaces.com/haunted_directories.htm#EVPbook

✓ **EVP and New Dimensions** (Paperback)
By Alexander MacRae (Author)

✓ **Communicating With the Dead** (Paperback)
By Jeff Belanger (Author)

✓ **Ghost Hunter's Guidebook: The Essential Guide to Investigating Ghosts
& Hauntings** (Hardcover) Troy Taylor (Author)

✓ **How to be a Ghost Hunter** (Paperback)
By Richard Southall (Author)

My Life and Experiences with EVP and Shadow People (Paperback)
By Alice Heaver (Author)

A Paranormal Glossary

It's all about Education

A

Absent Healing - Absent healing is done when you aren't in the presence of the person who needs the healing or in the presence of the person sending healing to you.

Afterlife - One of several terms used interchangeably to refer to life after death. The word "afterlife" has been used since 1615, and is generic enough to use in almost any setting and culture. Other terms include "crossing over," "the Otherworld," and "the other side." Most ghost hunters avoid specific religious terms such as "heaven" when discussing haunting, ghosts, and an afterlife.

Agent - A living person at the site of a haunting. Some human agents act only as witnesses to paranormal events while others are believed to be the method by which the haunting occurs. Some agents may cause phenomena to increase, while others may be the entire source of the activity. How this works is as yet still unexplained.

Akashic Records - These have become popular among people into the New Age movement. These are records stored in a place called Akasha of all experiences, past, present and future of every human being.

Altered State of Consciousness - Consciousness that is different from normal or transcendental to other realms or realities.

Amorphous - Having no definite form or shape, spirits and ghosts often appear in mist-like forms or shapes.

Amulet - Object charged with psychic power to ward off evil spirits; usually a charm worn around the neck.

Angels - A benevolent spiritual being that watches over and helps everyday people. They are spiritual beings that are here to help us. There is some debate as to whether these beings are purely Christian and of the Christian God or if these beings are here for anyone despite their religious affiliation.

Anniversary Haunting – Is a haunting that happens on the same day each year usually commemorating a traumatic or tragic event.

Anomaly - Something that is out of place and unexplained. In paranormal studies, it refers to any phenomena that we cannot explain. Example: A lens flare in a photo is not an anomaly, but an orb that we cannot explain is an anomaly.

Anomalies – Are more than one thing that is a deviation from what is considered normal by the masses.

Apparition - A spectral image that is sometimes referred to as a ghost, but is more like an imprint with distinct features that enables the witness to recognize it as a person or specific shape. They are usually connected to a residual haunting rather than spirit-related ones. Since the early 17th century, this refers to any ghost that seems to have material substance. If it appears in any physical form, including a vapor-like image, it may be called an apparition.

Apport - A physical object that can materialize and appear at will and can include coins, watches, jewelry and even food. They are often connected to spirits who interact with the living as the spirits cause items to appear and disappear in an effort to make them known.

Asport - A physical object that a spirit teleports to another location or makes disappear. The disappearance of an object or objects during a haunting that reappear again at a later time.

Astral Body - Soul of a person projected outside of their body; body of light; invisible spirit of a person or an animal; counterpart to the physical body that exists in the spirit realm. The part of you that leaves your body during an astral projection. Some people believe that it is your soul leaving your body.

Astral Plane - Another term for an out-of-body experience (OBE). It is believed there is a place called the astral realm where you can visit at will or most people go there accidentally and say they were dreaming. A world some people believe exists above the physical world.

Astral Projection - An out-of-body experience; Separation of the astral body from the physical body usually by a deliberate act of will.

Astrology - The theory and practice of the aspects of celestial bodies in the belief that they have an influence on the course of natural earthly occurrences and human affairs.

Attachment - A ghost is said to be "attached" when it manifest mainly in the presence of a certain person or object.

Aura - A field that some people and psychics see surrounding the living body, and inanimate objects; an energy field of light that surrounds living things and is believed to emanate from the astral body.

Autoscopy - Seeing one's "double", or looking back at one's own body from a position outside the body (OBE).

Automatic Writing - Writing without being aware of the contents, as when a medium apparently transcribes written messages from disembodied spirits. Automatic writing is done when in a trance like state. You write words, sentences, messages, etc. without being aware of the topic or of what is being written.

Automatism - Any unconscious and spontaneous muscular movement caused by "the spirits". (Such is the case with Automatic Writing).

B

Ball Lightning - A rare form of lightning in the shape of a glowing red ball that can last anywhere from a few seconds to several minutes. Typically associated with thunderstorms, these spheres are thought to consist of ionized gas.

Black Shuck - A spectral death omen in the form of a ghostly dog.

Banshee - From the Irish, bean sidhe, meaning female spirit. Her wail does not always mean death, and she does not cause anyone to die. She's generally not a ghost. Gaelic legend of an entity thought to announce the death of someone by groaning, wailing and screaming.

Benign Spirit - A spirit that is not considered harmful; One who is not causing any unrest or chaos.

Belief - Conviction or assumption; System of interpreting reality; Structuring thoughts or presumptions.

Bilocation - The appearance of someone to be in two separate places at the exact same time.

Bi-location - Being (or appearing) in two different places at the same time (similar to autoscopy). This is an alternate spelling of the word Bilocation.

Black Magic - Conjuring supernatural forces for a specific purpose using the aid of the dark powers. Using spells or rituals to intentionally cause harm to someone.

Bogey - Also referred to as the bogeyman in British folklore, these are classed as horrible or evil spirits that love to be mischievous. Sometimes synonymous with the devil, in the past the threat of calling upon the bogeyman was used by parents to frighten children into good behavior.

C

Call - A call is the response that is made by a subject during a card-guessing test or during any other type of ESP test.

Calling Ghost - These are ghosts that will call out the name of the living in order to get their attention.

Card Guessing – Is used as an experimental test for ESP in which a subject tries to guess the identity of a set of cards.

Cartomancy - A fortune telling technique done with playing cards.

Case Study - An in-depth investigation of an individual subject.

Channeling - The process by which a medium apparently allows a spirit to communicate through his or her person; allowing a spirit to communicate through a person; a form of voluntary possession.

Charm - A spell or object said to contain magical powers such as luck, religious help or black magic.

Circumanbulism Ceremony - Walking around an object or person to protect for it; proscribing a circle of protection.

Clairaudience - A sensitive said to be Clairaudient. Auditory form of ESP (compare with Clairvoyance); The ability to hear discarnate sounds and voices beyond normal hearing; psychic hearing. Obtaining information through hearing words or sounds from other world beings.

Clairgustance - A sensitive said to be Clairgustient. A psychic ability which enables someone to experience a sense of taste associated with a spirit.

Clairsentience - A sensitive said to be Clairsentient. Physical sensations (even smell) form of ESP. Sometimes used as a general term for clairvoyance and clairaudience; Person sensitive to psychic forces; persons who can easily sense feelings or emotions; even empathy.

Clairvoyance - A subset of ESP. The viewing of distant scenes not apparent to the eye, may appear externally - either replacing the normal visual scene (visions) or being incorporated into it (as could be the case with apparitions) - or internally, in the form of mental imagery and intuition. A person who can communicate messages from other realms without being in a trance like state.

Classic Haunting - The spirit of a once living person that for some reason did not cross over at the moment of death. A Classic Haunt involves a spirit that has the ability to interact with you and vice versa.

Cleansing - A less religious form of exorcism that is done to remove spirits from a location. Cleansing can be several different methods and rituals with burning sage, candles, incantations and prayers.

Closed Deck - A set of cards used in a card guessing deck in which each card will appear a fixed number of times. The statistical analysis obtained from a closed deck differs from that of an open card deck. (See also card guessing)

Cold Reading - Fraudulent reading by a psychic who uses psychological or historical clues to discern information. A technique commonly used by fake mind readers, mediums and magicians which allows them to obtain previously unknown information about a person by asking a general series of statements, questions and answers.

Cold Spot - An unexplainable drop in temperature associated with a paranormal event; cold or shivery sensation received when a spirit is nearby.

Collective Apparition - An unusual type of "ghost" sighting in which more than one person is witness to the same phenomenon.

Conjuring -The process of calling preternatural forces into aid or action through the use of Sorcery or ceremonial Black Magic.

Contagion - Contagion in paranormal research is when someone's impressions or data are influenced, consciously or unconsciously, by outside opinions or historical facts.

Contagion (Continued)-The act of being followed by a paranormal entity, such as an earthbound spirit from a haunted location.

Control - A spirit who acts as a medium's connection with the next world. Also referred to as a "spirit guide". This is also a procedure in paranormal psychology that ensures that the experiment is conducted in a standard fashion so that the results will not be influenced by any extraneous factors.

Control Group - A group of outside subjects whose performance or abilities are compared with the experimental subjects.

Clearing - or space clearing - Ridding an area of lingering unpleasant energy. It does not "kill" a ghost. Space clearing may encourage ghosts to cross over or at least leave the current haunted location.

Crisis Apparition - An out of body experience in which a person projects his or her astral body (or body of light) at a time of crisis or near-death The percipient is usually a family member or loved one.

Crystallomancy - The art of gazing into a crystal globe, a pool of water, a mirror, or any transparent object to see visions or summon forth spirits.

Curse - Invocation ritual to cause harm or injury to a person, place or thing.

D

Data Loggers - Digital data recorders that take continuous date and time stamped snapshots of several environmental conditions, including temperature, dew point, humidity and EMF.

Deep Trace Medium - A psychic who allows a spirit to enter their body so that the spirits can communicate through them. (Like Chris Fleming).

Déjà vu - The feeling of having experienced something before. An impression or dull familiarity of having seen or experienced something before. Many believe a spiritual sort of check point reassuring you and your spirit guide that you are on the correct path for your life.

Dematerialization - The sudden disappearance of a person or spirit in full view of a witness or witnesses.

Demonology - The research and study of Spiritual Demons and their bad habits. (From Greek δαίμων, daimōn, "demon";) is the systematic study of demons and others beliefs about demons. Demonology is an orthodox branch of theology. It is the study branch of theology relating to superhuman beings who are not gods.

Demons - An inferior deity often spoken of in religious text as pure evil.

Evil entity, hostile to humans; devilish spirit; Historically, this term has included deceased individuals. However, since the early 18th century, it usually refers to an evil spirit, sometimes more powerful than man, but less than Deity. Today, we generally do not use this term to indicate a deceased human being. The female demon, very rarely mentioned, is a demoness.

Dice Test - An experimental test in which a subject attempts to influence the fall of dice. This study is used for the investigation of psycho kinesis.

Direct Voice Phenomenon (DVP) - An auditory "spirit" or disembodied voice that is spoken directly to the sitters at a séance.

Discarnate - Energy or astral substance existing without a physical body; disembodied. A spirit that exists without a body.

Discernment - The ability to feel or perceive something with the use of the mind and the senses.

Disembodied Voice - An audible sound, word or conversation recorded or not, that does not have a known source. Audible to the human ear is VP. Audible only after being recorded is EVP.

Divination - The art of using objects or symbols to obtain information. Tools often used are tarot cards, etching, runes, reading tea leaves, etc.

DMILS - Abbreviation of Direct Mental Interaction with Living Systems. Used to denote instances where one person is attempting to influence a distant biological system, usually the physiology of another person. As it is unclear whether this represents an influence (see Psychokinesis), a case of ESP on the part of the influence (see ESP) or an opportunistic selection process, the term 'interaction' has been adopted.

Doppelganger - German word for "Double-Goer" or spirit double. A concept made popular in the early 19th century. A doppelganger is the apparition, or exact double, of a living person. Germans believe it means imminent death to meet your Doppelganger. It is an exact spirit double or mirror image of a person which is considered to be very negative.

Dowsing - Use of "L" shaped rods or forked tree branches to find "living" energy of water or spirits. May also be an ornate pendulum.

Dust Orb - Photographic orb caused by flash reflection off of invisible dust particles suspended in the air; generally small, non-pulsing white transparent circles; Large colored and/or pulsing (in videography) transparent circles are believed to be spirit movement.

E

Earthbound Spirit - Refers to a ghost or spirit that is unable to cross over at the time of death therefore stuck on earth. Many spirits make the decision to remain behind by choice while others are too confused or frightened because of a sudden death or suicide to make the crossing.

Ecstasy - An altered state of awareness where a person is experiencing great rapture and loss of self control.

Ectoplasm - Often referred to as "ecto," this is the physical residue of psychic energy. It's the basis for "slime" used in the Ghostbusters movies. Ectoplasm can be seen by the naked eye, and is best viewed in dark settings since it is translucent and tends to glow. It is very unusual. A thick fluid excreted by mediums when materialization is occurring.

Ekimmu - The legendary evil ghost of an individual who was denied entrance to the underworld and is doomed to walk the earth for eternity. Ekimmu means "that which is snatched away." One could become an Ekimmu by dying a violent death such as murder, drowning, or any other unsavory death.

Electronic Voice Phenomena - Ghostly voices recorded on audio or video tape; voices recorded on audio media that are only detected during playback; EVP; Call and response session. Voices and sounds from beyond that are captured and recorded on magnetic tape or digital sound waves.

Elemental - Primordial spirit or energy expressed in the elements of nature (Earth, Wind, Water, and Fire)

Elementals - Spiritualists commonly refer to this term to describe mean or angry spirits often also called "Earth Spirits".

Elemental Spirit - A spirit being associated with the four elements of the earth. (Earth, Air, Fire, Water).

EMF - Electro Magnetic Field, or Electro Magnetic Frequency. As the name suggests, it's a combination of electrical and magnetic fields. You'll find high EMF levels around power sources, fuse boxes, electrical outlets, computer monitors, microwave ovens, etc.

EMF Detector - (See Also Magnetometer) An instrument for measuring the magnitude and direction of a magnetic field typically used by paranormal researchers to detect a ghost's magnetic energy.

Empath - Sensitive person who can feel the energy or emotions of spirits or other living beings, human or animal.

Empathy - Rarely used in modern parapsychology, the popular usage of this term refers to a low-level form of telepathy wherein the Empath appears to be aware of the emotional state of a distant person. An Empath may also be able to "broadcast" emotions to others.

Entity - Any being, including people and ghosts, Disembodied or preternatural spirit; a being.

Era Cues - Also known as shanghai; the recreation of an era or period surroundings during an investigation; playing period music, vintage radio or television shows, playing recordings of a major event or a popular situation that occurred during the correlating time period. Everyday Paranormal's theory, that you can elevate paranormal activity from spirits of a certain era by presenting familiar pertinent stimuli from their time period.

ESP - Extrasensory perception. (receptive psychic) The ability to gain knowledge through means other than the five physical senses or logical inference. A sixth sense; ability to sense energy or information outside of the basic five senses of taste, touch, sight, sound and smell.

Ethereal - Heavenly or spiritual; not of this world.

Evil Eye - The evil eye has a long history. It is believed that someone with the evil eye ability can do things to you just by gazing at you. There are many, many charms and chants to chase away the effects of the evil eye.

Evocation - A chant or ritual to conjure up an entity. The summoning of spirits by usage of ritual, gesture, or verse of incantation.

EVP - Electronic Voice Phenomena, or the recording of unexplained disembodied voices, Voices and sounds that are alleged to be from the dead and that are captured by electronic mediums on tape or digital equipment. Ghostly voices recorded on audio or video tape; voices recorded on audio media that are only detected during playback.

Exorcism - A ritual used primarily by the Catholic Church as a way of driving out demons or evil spirits from a living person. Some fundamentalists also use this term to describe the expelling of spirits from a home or location. Expulsion of a ghost, spirit, demon, or other entity possessing human beings or a location; religious ritual to cast out evil forces.

F

Faeries - Usually, this means beings that live in the Otherworld or Underworld, parallel to our world and not far from it. Many people who readily accept the reality of ghosts don't believe in faeries.

False Awakening - An experience in which a person believes he or she has woken up, but actually is still dreaming.

False Positive - Paranormal evidence caused by a natural occurrence; common false positive is when cigarette smoke is captured on film, causing false ecto or mist.

G

Gauss Meter - A device that is used to measure the electromagnetic field, also referred to as EMF detectors or magnetometers.

Ghost - A sentient entity or spirit that visits or lingers in our world, after he or she lived among us as a human being. We've also seen evidence of ghostly animals and pets. An apparition or spirit that usually can be connected with a deceased person or animal.

Ghost Buster - Person or persons who attempts to rid a location of ghosts.

Ghost Hunt - Various methods of investigating reports of ghost and/or a haunting, to determine their authenticity.

Ghost Hunter - A person who attempts to find spirits and tries to document ghostly activity.

Ghost Investigation - Formal investigation of a place known to be haunted.

Ghostly Lights - Mysterious lights associated with accidents that have taken place near railroad tracks or roads; levitating lights that travel in straight light; unexplainable mountain lights; theatrical term for a light on a pole left on-stage while nobody is about. According to one tradition, theater owners leave the light on to keep the theatre ghost company overnight. If the ghost thinks it has been abandoned it could cause accidents to happen on the set.

Ghost Mist/Fog - This is a fog or mist that is visible on photographs but was not visible to the naked eye. A feeling of a presence, cold chill, smell, or phantom footsteps may be felt prior to capturing these phenomena on photos.

Ghost Ship - The appearance of a ship that has been known to have wrecked or disappeared years or even centuries ago to fore warn of a pending disaster.

Ghoul - Mistakenly used to mean a ghost, this word comes from the Middle East where it refers to an evil spirit that robs graves.

Glossolalia - More commonly known as "speaking in tongues". This can be anywhere from speaking a language that the person has never spoken before, to gibberish when in a trance like state.

Grey Lady - Ghost of a woman who has committed suicide over the loss of love or a lover; brides who commit suicide on their wedding day upon hearing the groom does not intend to marry them; pale and forlorn female apparitions dressed in a long white gown.

H

Hallucination - The perception of sights and sounds that are not actually present.

Haunted - Describes a setting where ghosts, poltergeists, and/or residual energy seem to produce significant paranormal activity. The word "haunt" originally meant to frequent.

Haunting - A repeated manifestation of supernatural phenomena in a specific location. The activity may appear as physical apparitions, sights, sounds, smells or cold areas. Hauntings may continue for many years or may only last for a brief period of time. Active visitation to a place by ghost; a place where ghosts or spirits seem to reside or to which they return.

Hellhound / Black Shuck - A spectral death omen in the form of a ghostly dog.

Hot Reading - A devious or fraudulent reading in which the reader has been given prior knowledge of the sitter.

Hot Spot - an area or place where witnessed frequent paranormal activity occurs, such as the appearance of spirits or ghosts, or disembodied voices and sounds.

Hypnosis - A technique that induces a sleep like state in which the subject acts only on external suggestion or can delve deeper into your subconscious for answers.

Hypnopompic State - Physiologically, sleep paralysis is closely related to the paralysis that occurs as a natural part of REM (rapid eye movement) sleep, which is known as REM atonia. Sleep paralysis occurs when the brain awakes from a REM state "after which the individual may experience panic symptoms and the realization that the distorted perceptions he or she had were false". As the correlation with REM sleep suggests, the paralysis is not entirely complete; use of EOG traces shows that eye movement can be instigated during such episodes. When there is an absence of narcolepsy, sleep paralysis is referred to as isolated sleep paralysis (ISP). In addition, the paralysis state may be accompanied by terrifying hallucinations (Hypnopompic or hypnagogic) and an acute sense of danger. Sleep paralysis is particularly frightening to the individual because of the vividness of such hallucinations. The hallucinatory element to sleep paralysis makes it even more likely that someone will interpret the experience as a dream, since completely fanciful, or dream-like, objects may appear in the room alongside one's normal vision. Some scientists have proposed this condition as an explanation for alien abductions and ghostly encounters. A study by Susan Blackmore and Marcus Cox (the Blackmore-Cox study) of the University of the West of England supports the suggestion that reports of alien abductions are related to sleep paralysis rather than to temporal lobe liability or reality.

I

Incubus - A demon posing as a male that is looking for or has had sexual intercourse with a living human woman. A demonic entity capable of sexually arousing and/or assaulting human women.

Indirect Voice - A spirit uses the medium to speak to whoever is in the room with the medium. Oftentimes, the voice coming from the medium is not the normal voice he or she has.

Infestation - Repeated and persistent paranormal phenomena.

Infrared thermometer – A non-contact digital thermometer measures surface temperatures by comparing the infrared energy to ambient energy.

Ignis Fatuus - A phosphorescent or spectral light that is alleged to be an indication of death. This phenomenon is thought to be caused by spontaneous combustion of gases emitted by rotting organic matter.

Illusion - A delusional perception between what is perceived and what is reality.

Intelligent Haunting - Activity that takes place around people or locations that is caused by an intelligent or conscious spirit. Best defined as the personality of someone who has died and whose spirit has not crossed over to the other side. This spirit will interact with the witnesses at a location and attempt to make its presence known through repeated phenomena of sights, sounds, feelings and the movement of physical objects.

Intuition - The act or faculty of knowing or sensing something without the use of the five normal senses; Non-paranormal knowledge that is gained though a perceptive insight.

Invocation - Summoning spirits by ritual, incantations or prayer.

K

Kinetic Energy - The ability to use pure energy to move objects.

Kirlian Photography - The method of using a type of camera that can take a picture that shows the complete aura of a person.

Kundlini - A vital energy usually manipulated in yogic practices that can provide energy to paranormal phenomenon.

L

Lepke - Finnish word (Lepke) used to describe a ghost that looks like a real person until it passes through a wall or does some other supernatural feat.

Levitation - Raising of a body or object into the air without any physical or visible means; ability to rise or hover above the ground.

Life Review - A flashback of a person's life that is typically associated with near-death experiences.

Life Force - Energy of life that animates the body and is the source of emotions, intelligence, personality, etc.

Linear Sweep - Involves placing data loggers in a straight line down a hall or stairwell. The data loggers take a reading every five seconds, so if any unknown entity were to pass through, the data loggers would capture it and record its exact movement.

Lucid Dreaming - A dream state in which one is conscious enough to recognize that one is in the dream state and is then able to control the dreams events.

Lycanthropy - The term used for the apparent transformation of a human being into a wolf.

M

Magic - Practice of causing changes to occur in conformity with will; sorcery.

Magnetometer (EMF, Gauss Meter) - An instrument used for measuring the magnitude and direction of a magnetic field. Typically used by paranormal researchers to detect a ghost's magnetic energy.

Malicious Spirit - A spirit that will destroy or damage things of personal or financial value for the sake of hurting others.

Manifestation - A witnessed physical appearance of a ghost, spirit, or event from a previously empty space.

Marian Apparitions - The event in which the Virgin Mary is seen.

Materialization - A witnessed sudden appearance of spirits in physical form; the sudden appearance of a person or object in front of a witness or witnesses.

Matrixing - When the mind attempts to manifest images as something they are not.

Meditation - The process of relaxing, emptying your mind of all thought or reaching a different state of consciousness. Meditation can aid in spiritual development and/or inner peace. There are many types of meditation. Private devotion or mental exercise consisting in any of innumerable techniques of concentration, contemplation, and abstraction, regarded as conducive to heightened spiritual awareness or somatic calm. It may serve purely quietist aims, as in the case of certain reclusive mystics; it may be viewed as spiritually or physically restorative and enriching to daily life

Metaphysics - Literally means beyond physics. Any unexplainable happenings that science can't explain or have a reason for happening are usually branched under this term.

Medium - A person who can communicate with spirits or ghosts; a person who acts as a conductor for spirit communication.

Mesmerism - A hypnotic induction of a sleep of trance state. (see also Hypnotism).

Miasma - A glowing mist usually sighted hovering above graves; miasmic light is a ghostly light.

Mist - Foggy or vapor-like materialization that can sometimes be traced to supernatural forces.

Malevolent - One wishing to do harm. A malevolent spirit wants to cause chaos and harm.

Motor Automatism - Bodily movement or functions that are accompanied but not controlled by consciousness. (see also automatic writing).

N

Nature Spirit - Elves, nymphs, dryads, sprites, and other nature spirits believed to be guardians of their environment.

Necromancy - The practice of conjuring spirits back from the dead.

Near Death Experience (NDE) - An experience that is reported by people who clinically die, or come close to actual death and are revived. These events often include encounters with spirit guides, seeing dead relatives or friends, life review, out-of-body experiences (OBE), or a moment of decision where they are able to decide or are told to turn back.

Neopagan - A follower of sympathizer of one of the newly formed Pagan religions based on ancient teachings or myths.

O

Occult - Means "Hidden". Pertaining to the preternatural or hidden principles behind nature; Hermetic. From the Latin, meaning something that is concealed or covered. Since the 16th century, it has meant anything that is mysterious. Today in America, it generally refers to magical, mystical and experimental studies.

Occultist - One who has "way better than average" knowledge of the Occult where spirituality comes into play. This does not mean an Occultist practices Occult beliefs. It is the study of those that do believe in occults.

Occultism - Esoteric systems of belief and practice that assume the existence of mysterious forces and entities.

Old Hag Syndrome - A nocturnal phenomena that involves a feeling of immobilization, suffocation, odd smells and feelings and is sometimes accompanied by immense fear (see also Sleep Paralysis).

Orb - Transparent or white ball believed to be spirit energy captured on film of trapped souls; can be caught on film, video tape, digital pictures, and sometimes seen with the naked eye; A round, whitish or pastel-colored translucent area in photos. Rarely seen in real life. Generally, these are perfectly circular, not oval. Many researchers believe that they represent spirits or ghosts. A photographed (not seen at the time of the photo) anomaly that, in theory, represents an ongoing "spirit" of a deceased person. It appears as a ball of light and may occasionally seem to be moving. This is a highly controversial subject since there are many reasonable circumstances that identify this as environmental (dust, rain, moisture in the air, dirty lens, insects, reflection, lens flare etc.). There has been no substantial proof that the balls of light are associated with "ghosts", "spirits" or any Paranormal behavior.

Ouija - From the French and German words for "yes," this is a spelling board used with a planchette'. A board pre-printed with letters, numerals, and words used by mediums to receive spirit communications. Usually a planchatte' (palm sized triangular platform) is employed to spell out words or point out numbers or letters. A game version of the Ouija board was mass-marketed as OUIJA by Parker Brothers in 1966 and is currently distributed by Hasbro. The device is intended to communicate with and through the spirit world, obtaining answers to questions. Many ghost hunters do not include them in scientific investigations, and some people object to them on principle alone. Most paranormal investigators, mediums and psychics do not recommend nor condone the use of Ouija Boards in investigations or just for fun. And I have seen a new Barbie Ouija Board for kids out on the market, great!

Out-of-Body Experience (OBE) - A sensation or experience in which ones self or inner spirit travels to a different location that their physical body. (see also Astral Projection).

Outward Manifestation - The physical manifestation of paranormal activity.

P

Paranormal - Beyond parapsychology, The prefix, "Para" indicates something that is irregular, faulty, or operating outside the usual boundaries. So, "paranormal" refers to anything outside the realm and experiences that we consider normal. Above or outside the natural order of things as presently understood; An event or person that is beyond the everyday experience or scientific explanation; out of the accepted norm of human experience. ; it also means the study of different forms of "normal" communication between beings.

Paranormal Investigation - The act of going to an alleged haunted location, to gather data such as photos, audio recordings, video, electromagnetic field monitoring, etc., and summarizing your data in reports.

Paranormal Researcher - Someone who uses their own theories/ideas to test new research methods, protocols, and equipment. A true researcher is not biased to an old idea, but works to disprove or prove further the old idea, to expand the knowledge of the community. Typically, a researcher does not work to prove a paranormal occurrence as genuine, but to disprove the occurrence legitimately. Only when all possible false-positive contaminants have been ruled out can something be defined as a true anomaly.

Parapsychology - A term coined by J.B. Rhine. The study of mental abilities and effects that are outside the usual realm of psychology. Parapsychology includes the study of ESP, ghosts, luck, psycho kinesis, and other paranormal phenomena; Scientific study of psychologically based phenomena beyond conventional explanation. The study of the evidence for psychological phenomena that is inexplicable by science.

Past Life Recall - To remember or have mental flashes about previous lives.

Pendulum - A small weight at the end of a cord or chain that is usually about six to ten inches long. The movement of the weight, when uninfluenced by other factors, can be used to detect areas of paranormal energy.

Pentagram - Magical diagram consisting of a five pointed star that is a representation of man; occultists consider it the most potent sigil for conjuring spirits. A pentagram is not the mark of the devil, it is a symbol used to protect us against Satan and all his demons.

Percipient - A person who sees (i.e., perceives) an apparition or ghost.

Phantasm - Projection of the mind; an illusion; sometimes used to connote a spirit or ghost.

Phantom - Another name for "ghost" or "spirit", although interestingly, many use the word "phantom" to refer to ghosts that have been seen wearing cloaks or robes; Any non-material spirit; specter, entity, or apparition; usually malevolent. Something that is seen, heard, or sensed, but has no physical reality. (also see ghost)

Phantomania - Paralysis that occurs when someone is under attack from supernatural or preternatural forces, also known as psychic paralysis.

PK - Movement of an object without using physical means; telekinesis; ability to move objects using the psychic or mental energy.

Planchette' - An indicator or pointer used in association with an Ouija Board, spirit board or talking board.

Poltergeist - From the German meaning "noisy ghost," this term has been in use since the early 19th century to mean a spirit that makes noise, or otherwise plays pranks often annoying. Unlike other ghosts, poltergeists can move from one location to another, following the person they've chosen to torment. Many psychologists believe that poltergeists are not ghosts at all, but some form of psycho kinesis or remote activity. A non-human spirit entity which literally means "noisy ghost" but is usually more malicious and destructive that ghosts of dead humans beings. Traditional poltergeists activities are thumping and banging, levitating or the moving of objects, stone throwing and starting fires. It is thought that poltergeist activity in some instances may be brought on subconsciously by an adolescent agent or females under the age of 25. The target human is called the epicenter and most if not all activity will be surrounding this person. Activity will escalate it the epicenter, (person) is agitated or scared.

Portal - Literally, a doorway or gate, this term suggests a specific location through which spirits enter and leave our world. When there are multiple phenomena in a confined area, such as an abundance of unexplained orbs, some people call this a "ghost portal."

Possession - A state in which a living person is taken over by a more powerful often malignant spirit or energy.

Premonition - A vision or feeling of some future event; a warning of approaching negative occurrence or occurrences in the future.

Precognition - The prior knowledge of future events. The ability to predict or have knowledge of something in advance of its occurrence, especially by extrasensory perception. (also see Clairvoyance).

Presence - The feeling that an unseen person, spirit or being is nearby.

Preternatural - Something that is associated with inhuman, primitive, demonic, or uncontrollable spirits or forces.

Protection - Objects, rituals, symbols, routines, tactics, or processes through which you guard yourself against psychic, demonic or paranormal intrusions and effects.

Psi - Popular term used to mean any psychic phenomena, psychic abilities, and sometimes inclusive of paranormal disturbances as well.

Also, a letter in the Greek alphabet that denotes psychic phenomena.

Psychic - From the Greek word meaning of the soul, or of life, this word usually refers to the world outside the domain of physical law. "Psychic" can relate to the spirit or the mind, depending upon the context. When someone is described as a psychic, it usually means that he or she is able to perceive things that are outside traditional physical laws and perceptions; A person who knows or communicates with unseen forces, spirits, or entities.

Psychic Attack - An attack that can either be physical or mental by a spirit.

Psychical - The popular British term used as an adjective or adverb, for what Americans call "psychic."

Psychokinesis (PK) - or psycho kinesis - To move something with the powers of one's mind, alone. It may be a factor in a haunting, and particularly in poltergeist phenomena. It's usually called "PK." The power of the mind to affect matter without physical contact, especially in inanimate and remote objects by the exercise of psychic powers.

Psychometry - The ability to acquire knowledge by touching an object associated with a certain person, place, thing, or time. The ability or art of divining information about people or events associated with an object solely by touching or being near to it. The ability to touch an object and "read" the imprints of energy attached to that object and tells about the history or owner of the object.

Pyrokinesis - The ability to unconsciously control and sometimes in rare cases produce fire with their mind only.

R

Radio Voice Phenomena (RVP)- A form of electronic voice phenomena received over a common radio in the AM, FM or short wave frequencies.

Reading - Information given to a person from the thoughts of a medium.

Reflection Image - A false positive that occurs when the flash of a camera reflects off of a shiny surface causing a false ghostly image or streak of light to appear on film.

Reciprocal Apparition - A rare type of ghost sighting when both the spirit and a human witness or witnesses see and respond to one another.

Reincarnation - The belief that each person possesses a soul which is independent of the body and can be reborn into another body after death.

Relic - An artifact or item closely associated with a saint or holy person, or some source of spiritual power.

Remote Viewing - Used by some psychics, this is a procedure in which the percipient or psychic attempts to become physically aware of the experience of an agent who is at a distant, unknown location though ESP.

Residual energy - Many ghost hunters believe that emotionally charged events leave an imprint or energy residue on the physical objects nearby. What distinguishes residual energy from an active haunting is that the energy/impressions repeat consistently, as if on a loop. The energy levels may increase or decrease, but the content remains the same with each manifestation. By contrast, in what we term an active haunting, the ghost may respond to environmental stimuli and direct contact; The energy behind classic anniversary hauntings; these cases exhibit a release of built up energy as if they were recorded in the walls or ground of a haunted location by some traumatic event; psychic imprint energy; spirit trapped in a continuous emotional loop in time.

Residual Haunting - Noises and or apparitions of people or inanimate objects, playing over and over as if stuck in the "play back" mode of a VCR. This "loop" is only a memory and will eventually fade with time. This is an unconscious spirit, incapable of an intelligent response. Communication would be futile.

Retro Cognition – An experience in which a person finds themselves in the past and is able to see and experience events in which they had no prior knowledge. Paranormal knowledge of past events.

RVP - A form of electronic voice phenomena received over a common radio in the AM, FM, short wave or microwave frequencies.

S

Satanic - Anything pertaining to Satan, the devil, his underlings and his worshippers.

Saturation - The first wave of a paranormal investigation, involving photographs and establishing baseline readings of environmental levels in the absence of perceivable paranormal activity.

Scrying - An umbrella term used to define methods of divination that may be considered forms of ESP. Some scrying methods include the use of water, dowsing rods, a crystal ball, flames of a candle, etc.

Séance' - A sitting that is held for the purpose of communication with the dead. At least one person in the circle is preferred to be a medium (or Psychic), with the power of contacting the spirits; A meeting or gathering for the purpose of contacting the dead; usually lead by a medium to receive spiritualistic messages, manifestations or communication with the dead at a table while participants are holding hands.

Sensitive - A person who possesses psychic abilities to sense the presence of energy from spirits, demons, or paranormal energy.

Shadow People - Shadow people are mysterious dark shadow in human form that appear in pictures or video, but may be invisible to the naked eye. It is thought that these spirits do not have enough energy to materialize as a full bodied apparition.

Shaman - A wizard, sorcerer, or medicine man in tribal societies who is an intermediary between the living, the dead, and the gods. One who practices

magic or sorcery for the purposes of healing, divination, and control over a natural event.

Shanghai - Also known as Era Cues; the recreation of an era or period surroundings during an investigation; playing period music, vintage radio or television shows, playing recordings of a major event or a popular situation that occurred during the correlating time period.

Shotgun Sweep - Placing digital data loggers though out a specific location (like shotgun pellets) to record changes in the environment that may indicate the presence of paranormal activity.

Simulacra - A word used to describe the faces and shapes that are often reported in photographs and in almost every kind of inanimate object including doors, buildings, clouds, trees and bushes. Usually, it is nothing more than the imagination of the witness making the texture of the object into a face or figure.

Sixth Sense - Extrasensory perception. (receptive psychic) The ability to gain knowledge through means other than the five physical senses or logical inference. A sixth sense; ability to sense energy or information outside of the basic five senses of taste, touch, sight, sound and smell.

Skeptic - A person who is yet undecided as to what is true. One who looks for rational explanations as to why something occurs.

Sleep Paralysis - A condition in which a person seems to be awake or conscious but is unable to move. (See also Hypnopompic)

Soul - The essence that distinguishes one person from another and survives through time. Your body is the host for a soul; a soul resides inside of every living being.

Sparkles - A visual effect described as the sparkle of embers falling immediately after a fireworks display. These small, sparkling lights will usually be present no closer to the camera than ten feet. They are often 20 to 50 feet away, or more. Some sparkles are seen during and especially immediately after the flash on a camera has been used for a picture. Even the most vivid sparkles will not show up on film. (If they do, check for dust or insects.) Sparkles are paranormal phenomena. "Sparkles" is a proprietary term developed in the 1990s by Fiona Broome during research for Hollow Hill. Other researchers have adopted the term to describe this unique phenomenon.

Specter (or Spectre) - Another term for a ghost; Phantom; disembodied spirit; grisly ghost; ghost not recognizable to the percipient.

Spirit - This word comes from the Latin, meaning that which breathes. It means that which animates life, or the soul of the being; Life force or human energy continuing to exist for a temporary period after death; a human soul after leaving the host body.

Spirit Photography - A term used for both legitimate attempts to capture ghosts and paranormal energy on film and also for the work of fraudulent photographers during the Spiritualist era. The art or process of taking photos using traditional film, or digital media to capture images of spirits.

Spirit World - Dimension of reality in which spirits reside Heaven, the Summerland, Valhalla, or more commonly, the Other Side.

Spiritualism - A faith based on the idea that life continues after death and that communication between the living and the dead can, and does, take place; Movement of belief in spirits and spiritual energy originating in the 1800s. The belief system that the dead are able to communicate with the living, through an intermediary or medium.

Stigmata - Unexplained bodily marks, sores, or sensations of pain corresponding to the exact locations of the crucifixion wounds of Jesus Christ.

Subjective Apparitions - Hallucinations of apparitions or other phenomena that are created by our own minds.

Subliminal Perception - Perceiving things without conscious awareness.

Succubus - A demon posing as a female that is looking for or has had sexual intercourse with a living human man. A form of Temptress or siren. A demonic entity capable of sexually arousing and/or assaulting human men.

Supernatural - Events or happenings that take place in violation of the laws of nature, usually associated with ghosts and hauntings; Pertaining to that beyond nature or above natural law; as opposed to the term "paranormal," the term "supernatural" connotes divine or demonic powers; Beyond or exceeding the laws of nature.

T

Talisman - Charm or drawing of various shapes and sizes that has specified purpose such as protection from good, evil, or good luck.

Talking Boards - A piece of wood bearing the letters of the alphabet that is used as a tool to make contact with the spirit world. Sitters place their fingers lightly on the planchette' or pointer, by which the spirits can spell out messages on the board. We do not condone the use of Talking Boards.

Tarot - The history of Tarot is still unclear. However, since its use in 14th century Italy, "Tarot" refers to playing cards that are also used for fortune-telling or divination.

Tarot Cards - A set or deck of (usually 72) cards that include 22 cards representing virtues and vices, death and fortune etc. used by fortunetellers to help them predict future events.

Telekinesis - From a Greek word meaning any motion that is activated from a distance. Technically, this could describe a remote-controlled toy boat, so we use the word psycho kinesis for our research; Movement of an object without using physical means; telekinesis; ability to move objects using the psychic or mental energy only.

Telepathy - Mental, non-verbal, or psychic communication between people. Communication between minds through means other than the five senses.

Teleportation - The appearance, disappearance or movement of human bodies and physical objects through closed doors or over some amount of distance using paranormal means. Such events often are reported to take place during hauntings; Dematerialization and re-materialization of an object; objects moved through time or space by supernatural forces.

Thermo scanner - Non-contact digital thermometer that measures surface temperatures by comparing the infrared energy to the ambient energy.

Thought Form - An apparition produced solely by the power of the human mind.

Tone Healing - Your tone of voice affects others by disturbing, catalyzing, soothing, lulling, inspiring and quite often healing them.

Trance - A hypnotic, cataleptic, or ecstatic state in which one becomes detached from their physical surroundings. Ability to tap into subconscious thoughts by placing yourself or someone else in an unconscious or relaxed sleep like state.

U

Unexplained EMF - Often indicate something paranormal. EMF fields can be measured with various tools, including an EMF meter or a hiking compass.

V

Vampire - Creature who, according to legend, feeds on human blood, and only walks at night.

Voice Phenomena - Also VP; Unexplained disembodied voices, Voices and sounds that are alleged to be from the dead and that can be heard audibly.

Ghostly voices witnessed by one or more persons, without the aid of digital audio equipment or recordings.

Vortex - Since the time of Descartes, this has indicated the rotation of cosmic energy around a central point or axis. Beginning in the mid-19th century, the word "vortex" has meant any whirling movement of energy or particles. In some circles, a misty vortex can mean an open spiritual portal for spirit travel; Energy tornado or tunnel of swirling spiritual energy; caught in photographs as orbs in motion; some believe them to be portals in time and space. An anomaly that appears as a funnel or rope-like image in photographs. These images are sometimes thought to represent ghosts, collections of orbs or gateways which travel to a wormhole in time-space. There has been no substantial scientific evidence to support any of these theories.

W

Warlock - Male witch; maverick witch seeking to destroy other witches.

Werewolf - According to legend, a person who transforms into a wolf or takes on wolf-like characteristics during a full moon.

White Noise - An acoustical or electrical noise of which the intensity is the same at all frequencies within a given band. A hiss-like sound, formed by combining all audible frequencies, often used as a background to EVP recordings.

Wicca - Witchcraft; A neo-pagan movement that honors the "Gods of Nature"; "Wicca" means "Wise One".

Witch - A female follower of traditional witchcraft or modern Wicca; person who harnesses forces of nature by conjuring spirits and spiritual energy.

Wraith - An apparition that when appears, is generally thought to be an omen of impending death.

Z

Zener Cards - A set or deck of cards for use in card-guessing tests for ESP. Zener cards were invented by Karl Zener.   Each set contains the following cards: a hollow circle (one curve), a Greek cross (two lines), three vertical wavy lines (or "waves"), a hollow square (four lines), and a hollow five-pointed star. There are 25 cards in a pack, five of each design.

In a test for clairvoyance, the person conducting the test (the experimenter) picks up a card in a shuffled pack observes the symbol on the card, and records the answer of the person being tested for extra sensory perception, who must correctly determine which of the five designs is on the card in question. The experimenter continues until all the cards in the pack have been used.

The shapes that appear on a set of Zener Cards

Index

EVP Lab 1.0

My Failures & Success in Recording

Electronic Voice Phenomenon

Dr. John D. Gruber Ph.D.

Made in the USA
Lexington, KY
16 March 2018